'STROLLER' WHITE
Klondike Newsman

'STROLLER' WHITE
Klondike Newsman

Compiled and edited by
R. N. De ARMOND

Cover illustration
"ELMER JOHN STROLLER WHITE"
Copyright © by Ted Harrison
October 1989

LYNN CANAL PUBLISHING
Skagway, Alaska

ISBN: 0-945284-03-9

Lynn Canal Publishing
P.O. Box 1898, 264 Broadway
Skagway, Alaska 99840-0498

Printed In U.S.A.

CONTENTS

FOREWORD

STROLLER WHITE III is the way my birth certificate reads. When my maternal grandmother first saw me a few days after I entered this world, she said, "Why he's not a Stroller, he's just a little toddler." So "Stroller" became "Toddy" became "Tod." It's funny how one man's spirited decision nearly a century ago to trek to the Klondike and a grandmother's witty comment 40 years later cause me to respond to "Hey, Tod!" today.

"Stroller," as a name, has had a curious history. *The* Stroller White, the original and the subject of this book, was known as Elmer John until he began a column called "Strolling Through The Yukon" in which he referred to the writer as "The Stroller." Thereafter, he was called Stroller by everyone (except by his wife, much younger than he, who always called him "Mr. White.")

Their son (my father) was born as Albert Hamilton in Whitehorse in 1906 and was always known as Albert, that is until he went to college in Washington where he informed one and all that his name was Stroller. Albert was no more, except to his mother who apparently had trouble keeping track of all these name changes.

Then a real honest-to-God officially certified Stroller finally arrived (me!) and you already know that story. But it continues. Our son, born more than a century after the original, is named Stroller Benjamin and has been called Ben all his life. That is until he went away to college where he informed one and all that his name was Stroller.

The newspaper tradition (which newspaper folks agree is genetic) lives on. Our daughter, Nadia, is a reporter and columnist for the *Stillwater Gazette* in Minnesota. Not quite the Yukon, but you can hear the iceworms chirp in February.

Growing up as the grandson of a fabled teller of tall tales of high adventure and low shenanigans who traded stories with the likes of Robert Service and Jack London, one might think that I was raised as a Klondike kid. I wasn't. Stroller (the 1st) was, as

vii

mentioned, much older than his wife — about 25 years. He was about 50 when my father was born. So my father was raised mostly by his mother who, being very athletic and active, taught him to hunt, trap, mountainclimb, handle the dog team and all the skills one needed there in those days. Together, they built a cabin on Auk Lake near Juneau in the shadow of Mt. Stroller White — long before that mountain took on that name (even the mountains become Strollers late in life!)

The tales my father told of his growing up in the Yukon and Alaska involved his mother much more than his father. Stroller was kept more than busy running the newspaper and with various civic activities (for a while, he was Speaker of the Territorial House of Alaska). Home life was, apparently, a bit on the quiet and formal side. After all, even his wife, who could, and frequently did, shoot and skin a bear, called him "Mr. White."

I recall two stories my father told about his father. One about mush, the other about cards. Every night, so I'm told, the Stroller would cook a pot of mush and every morning he wold fry it for breakfast. So what does this tell us? That he was helping with household chores before women's liberation made it fashionable? That his wife couldn't cook mush? That he balanced an otherwise hectic day by beginning and ending each with a routine as certain as the sunrise and sunset? I don't know. But I do know that I frequently begin my day with fried mush.

Playing cards was another passion (if you regard "mush" as a passion). My father had fond memories of countless nights counting 15-2, 15-4 in cribbage games with his father. This tradition, too, has been passed down. Dad and I played as regularly as my son and I now play — still using the mastodon ivory board that Stroller used in those early days.

I was thrilled when I first read Bob DeArmond's *Tales of a Klondike Newsman* in 1969. The stories told a lot not only about the highlights an low lifes of that great adventure, they told me a lot about my grandfather — his courage, tenacity, and great sense of humor. But, mostly, the stories caused me to realize how incredible it was that, surrounded by people who only wanted to strike it rich and move on, he was always a builder. When the others left, he stayed on. A very literate, civilized man, he had a different vision of the Northwest. He was committed to taming the frontier, to making it a place to live.

The book prompted our family to seek our roots. We visited Sitka, Juneau, Skagway, Whitehorse and Dawson in 1979. It was wonderful. Stories came alive as we walked Stroller's streets, visited the newspapers that are continuing what he started, and even bathed in the swiftly flowing Yukon — the icy "highway" he and his young family took from Whitehorse to Dawson.

But mostly we were impressed by the tremendous respect and affection that still exists for Stroller White. He is a legend, a greater hero than I'd ever realized. His contributions to the folklore and development of the Yukon and Alaska are certainly not forgotten and I doubt they will be — thanks to the efforts of people like Bob DeArmond and Jeff Brady.

Jeff was publisher of *The Skagway News* when we visited in '79. When I dropped in and introduced myself, he was so flabbergasted at having a real Stroller White in his office that he called a special meeting of the Eagles. The Eagles was a club formed by respectable citizens of Skagway during the gold rush days to try to maintain law and order. Stroller was a charter member. Jeff Brady and other currently respectable citizens of Skagway have resurrected the Eagles Club to, among other things, keep alive the memory and irreverent humor of the Stroller. Behind closed doors and after, I'm sure, heated debate, they decided to vote me in as an honorary member.

I can think of no greater honor the "respectable citizens" of Skagway could have bestowed upon Stroller White than to accept a total stranger from New Jersey into their very elite club simply because his name was Stroller. I was deeply touched.

Thank you, Jeff and special thanks to Bob DeArmond for creating this new edition to get more people "Strolling Through The Yukon."

— Stroller Tod White
Princeton, New Jersey
October 1989

INTRODUCTION

SWEPT NORTHWARD with the great tide of the Klondike Gold Rush at the end of the last century was an assortment of newspapermen, poets, writers and would-be writers. Some were working reporters who had been assigned by metropolitan newspapers or magazines to cover the big event. Joaquin Miller, T. C. Dunn, Hamlin Garland, A. A. Hall and Frederick Palmer were in this group and after writing their stories they did not tarry long in the North but went elsewhere to continue their work.

A very few — perhaps it should be limited to Rex Beach and Jack London — eventually gained literary fame, but they also soon left the country. Dozens of other men, and a few women, who were not writers by trade, did write and publish accounts of their own adventures in the Klondike. Many of these accounts are interesting and historically valuable, but their authors, for the most part, did not settle down and become residents, either.

Out of the whole flock of word-mongers who joined the big rush between 1897 and 1900, few more than a double handful of the newspapermen remained in the North and became a part of it. Roy G. Southworth, George Lafayette Bellows, Will and Harry Steel, John F. A. Strong, W. F. Thompson, O. W. Dunbar, John W. Troy, George B. Swinehart, E. S. Bunch, Elmer J. White, Robert J. McChesney, George M. Arbuckle, Eugene C. Allen and Zach F. Hickman are names that come to mind. These men were reporters and editors at Skagway or Dawson, or both, during the height of the Klondike boom, and later they drifted on to Nome and Fairbanks and other Alaska gold camps and towns. Some of them settled down in one place, others roamed from one camp to another, but whatever the location they wrote thousands and thousands of words about the North for the news and editorial columns of their respective papers.

Their writing varied as to style but the content was pretty much the run of the news mill. They wrote about the everyday happenings and the special events of their regions, including the stampedes and gold strikes, the floods, fires, blizzards, steamboat wrecks and other disasters, social events and business and politics, and they offered editorial comment on affairs of local, territorial and national interest.

Except for one of their number, however, the thing they did not write about in their papers was the Klondike Rush, the most spectacular happening that has yet taken place in the whole vast region. Just why they did not write about it is a matter for speculation. Perhaps, having lived through it, they preferred to forget about it. Or they may have regarded the subject as so familiarly experienced in the lives of readers that they would not be interested. It seems most likely, however, that they were just too busy with the day-to-day grind of producing newspapers to find the time or energy to reminisce in writing. Whatever the reason, our literature is the loser for their failure.

The exception was a man named Elmer J. White, commonly known as "Stroller" White, whose writings were probably the most widely read and copied of any in the North. "Stroller" White is believed to have been the Northland's first newspaper columnist, as that term is understood today, and if he was not the first he certainly was by far the most enduring one ever to appear on the northern scene.

His column, "The Stroller," first appeared in the *Klondike Nugget* at Dawson at least as early as 1900. During the next thirty years it appeared primarily and successively in the *Dawson Free Lance*, the *Whitehorse Star*, the *Douglas Island News* and *Stroller's Weekly*, and it appeared secondarily, at least now and then, in nearly every newspaper in Alaska, making "Stroller" White far and away the most quoted newspaper writer and "The Stroller" the most copied newspaper feature in the entire North.

"Stroller" White owned all of the above mentioned papers except the *Nugget* and he made his weekly column an entertaining feature, leaving such serious subjects as politics, in which he was keenly interested, to the straight editorial columns which adjoined the feature. And, in addition to "The Stroller," for many years he produced a weekly "Bedtime Stories for Alaska Children."

In "The Stroller" he reminisced about his early years, first on a farm in Ohio and then as a newspaperman in the Deep South, addressed open letters of homespun advice to every President of the United States from Theodore Roosevelt through Calvin Coolidge, propounded Rube Goldbergian inventions to cure or prevent snoring and other afflictions, advised the lovelorn — both single and married — and concerned himself with the plight of knee-sprung sales girls and other unfortunates.

And every now and then, and particularly in his later years, "Stroller" White spun a yarn or dredged up an anecdote about Gold Rush Days in Skagway and Dawson, or wandered off into recollections of the people he had known in those gaudy years when, in his words, the whole Northland was in bloom. In 1910, shortly after he started the *Iditarod Pioneer,* George M. Arbuckle "lifted" one of these Klondike anecdotes from the *Whitehorse Star* and by way of introduction wrote: "Elmer White, with whom this scribe labored on the *Bennett Sun* nearly a dozen years ago, is rapidly getting to be for the Rush of '98 what Bret Harte was for the California Rush of '49. Let there be more of the same."

Mr. White responded in typical fashion: "George M. Arbuckle, who became known to fame as 'The hired hand of The Bennett Sun,' has paid The Stroller a very pretty compliment, which The Stroller appreciates. In the past four years 'Buck' has had his printing plant on steamboats more than half the time during the open season, having operated at Chena, Cleary, Fairbanks, Manley Hot Springs, Innoko, Gibbon and now, Iditarod City. Really, it is time for 'Buck' to settle down."

Elmer White may have been more settled, in his younger days, than was 'Buck' Arbuckle, but not much more. He was born near Cambridge, Ohio, on November 28, 1859, and grew up on a farm there. "The Stroller knows what it is to have barley beards down his neck and up his pants legs — a long way down, and a long way up," he once wrote. And it may have been another aspect of the farmer's life that caused him to abandon it. "A farmer might as well sell his bed and blankets about the first of April," he wrote, "because he will have no more need of them until after the harvest is in, along toward Thanksgiving time."

At any rate, after graduating from Muskingum College at New Concord, Ohio, White headed for Florida to begin his newspaper career on the *Gainesville News.* During the next ten years he worked as the trade in Florida and Georgia. At some time during those years he married and had a son, John McBurney White, but the marriage apparently terminated before 1889 when he moved west to Washington Territory. There he worked on a number of papers in the Puget Sound area and in December, 1891, he married Miss Josephine Keys at Tacoma. A daughter, Lenore, was born to them in Washington.

In the spring of 1898, when the rush to Dawson was building toward its peak, White journeyed north to Skagway where he worked for the *Skagway News*. His family joined him during the summer and in the fall they started for Dawson, stopped briefly at Bennett for a stint on the *Sun,* and made the trip down the Yukon from Whitehorse on a scow. In the "Queen City of the Klondike" White worked for the *Klondike Nugget* and the *Dawson Daily News* and perhaps for other papers before he started his own *Dawson Free Press* in October, 1903. He continued this paper for about six months, then moved to the southern Yukon and took over the *Whitehorse Star* which he changed from a weekly to a daily paper. Whitehorse however, was not yet large enough to support a daily, and in 1906 the *Star* reverted to a weekly.

A son, who was named Albert Hamilton, was born to Mr. and Mrs. White at Whitehorse and they continued to live there until the spring of 1916 when they returned to Alaska and settled at Douglas. "Stroller" White took over the weekly *Douglas Island News* just a year before the great Treadwell Mine, the mainstay of the town's economy, caved in, flooded, and shut down.

In 1918, the year following that disaster, Mr. White filed as a Democrat for a seat in the House of Representatives of the Alaska Territorial Legislature and was elected. He was also elected Speaker of the House when the legislature convened at Juneau in the spring of 1919. After the session ended he was appointed the first Director of the Alaska Bureau of Publicity and he held the position until it was abolished by the 1921 legislative session.

By that time the population of Douglas had shrunk drastically and Mr. White was reluctantly forced to close the newspaper. He moved the plant across the channel to Juneau and began publication of *Stroller's Weekly*. He continued to publish this paper until his death, which occurred at Juneau on September 28, 1930. During the time he lived in Juneau he also served as a member of the Alaska Historical Library and Museum Commission. An imposing mountain peak near Juneau today bears the name Mount Stroller White.

Following Mr. White's death, Mrs. White continued to publish *Stroller's Weekly* for some months, during which this writer worked on the paper. It was then sold and became first the *Alaska Press,* then the *Alaska Daily Press,* and finally, before its demise, the *Alaska Sunday Press.*

As was mentioned earlier, Mr. White began publishing his column, "The Stroller," in the *Klondike Nugget* at Dawson. He continued it in all of his other papers and one of them, the *Whitehorse Star,* still runs a department with that name although it is now devoted to personal news items rather than feature material.

I have had opportunity to read only a scattering of "The Stroller" columns that appeared in the Dawson and Whitehorse papers, but from those I have seen I have gained the impression that Mr. White did not write a great deal about Gold Rush days until after 1916, when he moved to Douglas. I have read all of his feature columns that appeared in the *Douglas Island News* and in *Stroller's Weekly,* covering a period of more than fourteen years. The reminiscences of the big Rush and the Klondike are scattered through the weekly columns of all those years.

"Stroller" White concerned himself little, in these writings, with formal history or with the people who struck it rich or in other ways gained fame. For the most part he wrote about the ones he called "the Sam brothers, Flot and Jet," and all their kinfolk — the gamblers, bartenders, and dancehall girls, and the drifters and ne'er-do-wells who were less interested in exercising the business end of a No. 2 shovel in search of gold than in rounding up three squares a day without working for them. About these people he wrote with perception and humor, and as with all true humor, his variety contained sizeable grains of truth. But he left social criticism to others and rarely condemned his bums and vagrants or their ways of life. In this respect his interests and his writings resemble those of another news-paperman who gained a good deal of fame with his chronicles of another sleazy set, the incomparable Damon Runyon.

From time to time in his columns "Stroller" White announced that he would one day write a book. He never did, or at least no book manuscript has come to light. Had he written the book, it would likely have concerned Gold Rush days as he saw them, and this compilation is an effort to supply that material. The tales here presented are drawn from "The Stroller" columns that appeared in the Douglas and Juneau papers, plus a few writings in other newspapers and in the *Pathfinder,* a monthly magazine that was published by the Pioneers of Alaska, a fraternal order.

The word "tales" was selected deliberately, in view of one of its several definitions: "An account of some event or sequence of events, actual, legendary, or fictitious." Just how the cataloguers will classify this collection I am not sure, because some of the tales are wholly factual, as nearly as any reporter can gather and write the truth of a happening; others are entirely fictional, and many are a combination of fact and fiction. All together they present, accurately I think, views of Klondike Days that have not previously appeared outside the newspaper columns.

— R. N. DeArmond

PREFACE TO THE REVISED EDITION

IT IS NOW very nearly sixty years since Elmer J. "Stroller" White passed from the Alaska-Yukon scene, the scene that he observed so keenly and wrote about so penetratingly in the columns of his various newspapers. In those writings he was able to leave us pictures of some of the colorful variety of people who sojourned in the Northland in those gaudy days following the Klondike discovery.

Seven new chapters have been added to this second edition, and an eighth was rewritten with some new material. All of the Stroller's writings in the first edition were culled from two of his papers, *The Douglas Island News* and *Stroller's Weekly.* Most of the material that has been added to this edition is from an earlier time, when the Stroller was writing first for *The Klondike Nugget,* and later when he was publishing his own paper, *The Whitehorse Star.*

There is less from the last-named paper than I would have liked to have. When I went to gather the material from the microfilm files at the Yukon Archives in Whitehorse, I discovered that at some distant time, before they were filmed, someone had carefully torn out the quarter-page occupied by "The Stroller" in most editions of the paper. Somewhere there may exist a full and unblemished file of *The Whitehorse Star.* I hope so. Those missing columns are a sad loss to the literature of the North.

— R. N. DeArmond
December 1989

THE STROLLER COMES NORTH

LIKE A FRESHLY hatched bumblebee, Skagway was full grown very young in life, and the town, less than a year old, was full of buzz and bumble and a lot of other things when the Stroller landed there in the early spring of the year 1898. During the next several months Soapy Smith and the Stroller held services in Skagway, each in his own separate and distinct manner. Soapy operated with three shells and a small pea and used automatic artillery, while the Stroller conducted a mild-mannered newspaper in which he pointed out the rewards of upright living and urged his readers always to put a squirt of lemon in it. Soapy worked on a cash basis while the Stroller extended credit, some of which is still extended.

Skagway is where much of the history of the Gold Rush was written, and where a great deal more history was made but never written. It is the Stroller's intention to put down in this department of his newspaper, now and then and as the spirit moves him, some of that previously unwritten history, not only of Skagway but also of Dawson, in the heart of the Klondike, and to tell about some of the people he met and associated with in those halycon days when the Northland was in bloom.

But before he launches into this program of uplifting history and moral entertainment, the Stroller should introduce himself to his new readers and explain to them how and by what means he came to the Northland in those early and glittering days of the Klondike Rush. The Stroller had the great good fortune to be born on a farm in Ohio, and the even greater good fortune to escape from the farm at an early age. After several years of being herded with the cows and of burning his bed every spring so he could devote his full time to herding a plough down a long furrow, he left the farm. He has never returned to it. Nor does he ever intend to return to it.

At the age of twenty-two, the Stroller went to Florida with the idea of reconstructing the unregenerate South. For a time he engaged in keeping school — and the word "keeping" is used advisedly instead of "teaching." Later he sank into the newspaper business as a means by which to reach more people with what he was then pleased to term "moral uplift." For six years he conducted a newspaper, drank moonshine whiskey, ate pie with a knife and in many ways contributed to the gayety of nations and endeared himself to the common people.

Looking back on his work in Florida, the Stroller points with pride to two reforms worked by him. When he began his ministrations it was estimated that in the county where he was located some 14,000 dogs slept in beds with their owners. When he left there half a dozen years later, the number had been reduced to 9,876. The other accomplishment was that the leading and most influential drunkards in the Stroller's community were acting upon his advice and putting a squirt of lemon in it.

From Florida the Stroller came to the Pacific Coast. Before he had been six months in the territory of Washington it had become a sister in the Sisterhood of States, and has been prospering ever since. While the Stroller does not take all the credit for making Washington a state, the fact remains that it had been a territory for a long time before he entered it.

2

In Washington the Stroller acquired a wife and gave up eating pie with a knife — in that order. He still retains both of these habits, being a charter and dues-paying member of the Same Old Wife Society and making minimum use of the knife when he is out in society. After nine years in Washington it began to look as though the Stroller was settled for life and would remain there, and he was content — at least reasonably content. Then one morning in the summer of 1897 the steamer *Portland* arrived at Seattle with what was billed in the newspaper headlines as a "Ton of Gold from the Klondike." Actually, the total was closer to two tons, but one ton created excitement enough. The rush to the Klondike gold fields began almost at once, and simultaneously the Stroller developed a severe case of itch in his pedal extremities. He tried plasters, ointments, salves and unguents; he soaked his feet in cold water, hot water, lukewarm milk and Budweiser with an egg in it. Nothing helped. The itch grew worse instead of better, and by the following spring he could stand it no longer. His feet were killing him, and the only cure was to get them moving, northward.

Thus it was that the Stroller boarded a rickety little wooden steamer one fine morning in Seattle. Passenger space was at a premium and the Stroller felt fortunate to be aboard. That is, he felt fortunate until it was too late for him to turn back. The vessel had been built originally as a tug, and after the start of the Gold Rush she had been remodeled to carry passengers. She was fitted up to take about twenty passengers in fair comfort, the Stroller would judge, and there were   seventy-six aboard when she sailed from Seattle. It was her maiden voyage in the passenger trade and it was the Stroller's maiden voyage on the briny deep. The boat had sailed, after her remodeling, without undergoing any trial runs, so had the Stroller, and the trip was more or less of an experiment all around.

3

Just about everything went wrong that could go wrong. The caulkers must have missed a few of the seams and the pumps had to work continuously to keep her from sinking. When the engine was humming along smoothly, the steering gear went on the blink, and after it was fixed, the engine pulled a strike. There were head winds all the time and the water didn't stay flat and smooth but kept humping up and swishing around in a manner that was very disconcerting to the Stroller and most of the other passengers. The gangplank washed overboard and was lost and so many things happened that the officers began to declare that one of the passengers must be a hoodoo.

We had been alternately drifting and steaming for the best part of a week and had reached a point near the north end of Vancouver Island, about a third of the total distance to be covered, when the jinx was discovered one evening while we were at dinner. One of the passengers was a great lummox of a fellow from Pittsburgh who wore a fur coat that must have cost $150 and whose entire luggage consisted of suitcases and trunks full of fancy dress clothing. He had a mouth like a dredge bucket and he generally stood around with it wide open as though set for flies, and the other passengers did not much take to him. On this particular evening the water was smoother than it had been and soup was served at dinner for the first time. The way that fellow went after the soup with his dredge bucket was instructive to watch and marvellous to hear. The captain, who was seated on the opposite side of the dining saloon, stopped eating when the Pittsburgher made his first intake. The captain looked and listened, then he started toward the sound, which resembled that of a hard-working freight engine. There was no doubt in the mind of the captain — any man who consumed soup with such a resounding intake would put a jinx on a battleship, let alone a frail, done-over tugboat. The captain ordered the

4

Pittsburgh man confined to his room for the rest of the voyage and threatened that any flunkey caught carrying soup to him would be put in irons.

"Talk about whistling up a wind," the captain was heard to say as he returned to his dinner. "It's a wonder we didn't have a hurricane."

Well, the wind died down at once, the water flattened out, and from then on all of the machinery hummed along as though it had never had an ailment in its life. It is true that the leaks did not stop, but at least they got no worse and the trip was completed without difficulty or delay. The Stroller makes no attempt to explain this; he merely recites the facts as he observed them. And while he is not superstitious, the Stroller has often thought of that incident because he later on ran across the Pittsburgh man in Skagway. It was this way:

The fellow landed at Dyea with his trunks and suitcases and within a few days he contracted a severe case of cold feet. In fact, he decided he had seen all of the North he wanted to see. He sold his entire outfit, including the fur coat and all the other clothes except those he wore, for $200 and headed for Skagway to catch a boat south. But in Skagway, Delilah saw him coming, and took him in. Delilah, in fact, had taking ways, and two nights later the Stroller saw the fellow in the alley next to the Red Onion Saloon. He was weeping copiously and he knew not where to lay his head. He was staked to the price of a meal and spent the night on the floor of the printing office where the Stroller had secured employment. The office had been carelessly built and the floor was corrugated like an old-fashioned washboard, but it was better than sleeping in the street. The next morning the Stroller got the fellow a job shoveling coal for his passage on a steamer going to Seattle. This was easily done as many crew members were deserting their ships as soon as they reached Skagway. But the

Stroller thoughtlessly neglected to warn the captain of the steamer and he supposes that the Pittsburgher got hold of some soup. At any rate, when the steamer was crossing Queen Charlotte Sound on her way south she lost her rudder and nearly drifted on the rocks before she was taken in tow by another vessel.

On that trip north in the spring of 1898 the Stroller was going to Skagway where he hoped to and did secure a newspaper job, but the other seventy-five passengers were headed for Dyea, a few miles beyond Skagway and at that time the preferred gateway to the Interior. Those passengers, seventy-four men and the wife of one of them, were a fair cross-section of the thousands who were then pouring northward, and that means they were a somewhat motley assortment. The Stroller will not attempt to describe all of them but will mention a few who carved for themselves a niche in his memory.

Only one man of the whole lot had previously been in the North, and he was a great disappointment to the others. He had been sent out to St. Michael in 1896 by the Alaska Commercial Company to work in its trading post there and had remained until the fall of 1897 when he returned to his home in California for a visit. Now he was on his way to Dawson to work for the same company. He wore a seal skin coat and was dubbed the "Seal Skin Kid" by the other passengers and plied with every imaginable question about the Klondike and gold mining. When he replied that he had never been within a thousand miles of the gold fields and knew nothing about them except what he had read in the papers, he was set down as either a fraud or a tightwad who wished to keep the inside track by hoarding his knowledge. Actually, he was an honest man. Had he been otherwise he could have peddled wild tales and misinformation by the bushel and it would have been swallowed greedily and with gratitude. But he was honest and the other passengers were disappointed and soon left him alone.

Another of the passengers was a Texan, past middle age, who stood at the rail of the steamer by the hour, twirling a six-shooter on his forefinger and firing out across the water on each twirl. The shots were so close together as to be almost continuous until all six had been fired. The performance gained him a lot of admiration from the other passengers — from a safe distance. They considered him hard-boiled and kept away from him. Later on in Skagway the Stroller learned that he was a member of Soapy Smith's gang who had been delayed in joining his chief. The Colorado penitentiary had not released him until the previous week.

Then there was a big corn-fed galoot from Iowa who had a suitcase full of playing cards and poker chips. He claimed to have acquired special skills, of which he was exceedingly proud, in a room back of the cigar store in his native village and he had, he said, a system that could not be beat. He was coming north to make a killing in a short time. Something must have gone wrong with the system because within a month, after trying both Dyea and Skagway, he shipped out as deckhand on a lumber schooner that expected eventually to get back to Puget Sound. He had lost his money, the cards, the chips and the suitcase, and he announced that if he ever got his feet on Iowa soil again he would keep them there.

All of the other passengers on that little boat were heading for the Klondike as fast as they could get there, and all were confident that all they would have to do when they got there was to scoop nuggets into a sack. There were long and solemn arguments as to whether it was best to hold the sack with the left hand and shovel with the right, or the other way around, while some thought it would be better to team up in pairs and take turns shoveling and holding.

But of the lot of them, the only ones the Stroller ever saw, with or without sacks, after he reached Dawson were the Seal Skin Kid and an Englishman named John Henry Littlejohn. The Seal Skin Kid stayed in Dawson for two years, then returned to California where, the last time he was heard of, he was married and raising a family. The Englishman, John Henry Littlejohn, will be mentioned again by the Stroller later on. All the others disappeared, swallowed up by the hordes of eager gold seekers or turned back by one form of adversity or another.

As for the little ex-tugboat that brought the Stroller to the Northland, she continued to ply between Puget Sound and Alaska for another six years and was then lost with all hands. She sailed from a Southwest Alaska port one day in 1904 and has not since had need of her gangplank, never having reached a port where a gangplank was required. The Stroller has often thought about her and wondered whether the unfortunate craft shipped another soup-inhaler, or whether the old jinx came to life after all that time.

SKAGWAY
1898

IT WAS IN THE dapple iron-gray of early morning that the Stroller first saw Juneau, after he had scrambled ashore from the little wooden steamer that was carrying him north to Skagway. The windows of heaven were open and likewise the floodgates, and the ensemble was not fair to look upon nor to loiter around in. The Stroller remembers that what little of the town he could see through the downpour was rather uninviting and he noticed that there seemed to be more paint on cheeks and lips than on buildings. But ten hours later he arrived in Skagway and was sorry he had not decided to remain in Juneau.

The landing at Skagway was made at a long wooden pier that poked itself out over the tideflats at the head of Lynn Canal. It seemed to the Stroller, as he trudged along it in the dank atmosphere of late evening and early spring and carrying his meagre luggage, that it was at least a mile long, although he later found that it was less than half that length. The closer he got to the town, the less he liked what he could see and hear of it as it seemed to be mostly tents, shacks, shanties and noise. The Stroller did not particularly look for sober men, but he did not see any that he remembers, although he presumes there may have been some around since it was still an hour or two short of midnight. But the Stroller was weary and as he did not care to size up the town until he could do so in daylight, he entered the first hotel he came to and, with an optimism born of crass ignorance, asked the man behind the desk for a room. What he had in mind was a single room or, in case of extremity, sharing a double.

"We have a room," said the man. "Gimme a dollar and go up both flights of stairs. The room is at the top of the last flight. Take the first bed that isn't occupied."

The Stroller followed instructions, found a cot just inside the door of the room mentioned, rolled into it and went to sleep. He slept soundly; indeed, he slept so soundly that he did not hear any of his seventy-eight roommates as they came in. But that was the number he counted, in the dim light that trickled through a small and grimy skylight, when morning came. There were tiers of bunks four deep around the walls, while the entire floor space, which was big enough for a skating rink, was thickly sprinkled with cots. All of the bunks and cots were occupied and since most of the occupants were packers and mule-skinners and longshoremen who were busily engaged in wooing Nature's sweet restorer after many hours of hard and sweaty toil, the Stroller noticed an atmosphere about the place he had never previously encountered. Neither has he encountered it since; nor has he searched for it. Before the next night the Stroller moved into a printing office where he slept on a mattress under the press.

From the "hotel" the Stroller went in search of breakfast and he had his first meal in Skagway in the International Cafe for Ladies and Gentlemen. It was a shack about half as long as its name just off the sidewalk at the corner of Broadway and Fifth Avenue and it was operated by an old San Francisco newspaperman and his wife — at least, he said she was his wife. The food was plain and good, and it was plentiful. But while the Stroller was at work on his hot cakes an Irishman entered and was about to take a seat at the counter. Before he sat down he noticed a placard on the wall and he immediately turned and started for the door.

"That," said the Irishman, "is what druv me from home,"

10

and he pointed to the placard, which read: "Coffee Like Your Mother Used to Make."

And speaking of restaurants, there were scores of them in Skagway at that time, for thousands of transients were moving through on their way to the gold fields and they remained in town anywhere from one day to several weeks. Prices at the restaurants were reasonable. A square meal at a bare board place could be had for twenty-five cents; bare boards and paper napkins were rated at thirty to thirty-five cents, while tablecloth and real napkin places ran from forty to fifty cents. An exception was the Pack Train Restaurant, which deserves and will receive special mention later. Its tables were bare at that time, although it furnished paper napkins, and its meals ran from twenty-five cents up to fifty cents and even higher for special dishes.

Most of these eating places changed hands frequently, their owners being almost as transient as the customers they served. This was because hundreds of people had started for the Klondike with outfits of grub to last a year, and after landing in Skagway many of them were attacked by what was known as icicle feet. In order to get as much from the outfit as possible — or at least enough to take them back home — they pitched tents or threw together board shacks and opened restaurants. If they took in enough money the first day to pay the fare back to Seattle, they often sold out for anything that was offered.

The Stroller remembers one restaurant that he patronized briefly because it was handy. It opened early one morning next door to the printing office and by mid-morning its proprietor had peddled enough hot cakes to buy a ticket for Seattle. He sold out to another fellow who kept it through the lunch hour, then sold it to a third party. The third owner served dinner, after which he got into a game of seven-up with one of his customers and lost the place. The

11

Stroller did not return to that restaurant to learn what happened thereafter. As Mark Twain once said, there was too much variety in it for him.

Immediately following his first breakfast in Skagway, the Stroller set out to look over and size up the new town in which he had landed. Skagway then had a population of somewhere between eight and ten thousand, counting those who would stop and look around when anyone yelled, "Hey, Kid." There were between 500 and 750 of these "Kids," each with his special designation, and about an equal number of — well, they wore skirts when they wore anything at all, did singing and dancing acts on the various stages and entertained in the numerous dancehalls, and if they were not of the demimonde, as the Stroller understands that term, they were closer to it than a strict interpretation of the law allowed.

At that time, in the first half of the year 1898, wives and children were scarce in Skagway and the result was that a great deal of affection was stored up to expend on them when they should finally arrive. Also, it was by no means uncommon for the storage tanks to spring a leak, there being plenty of opportunity for acquiring punctures of that nature. But by the middle of that summer every steamer came laden with women and children. When a steamer whistled in the bay it was not unusual to see two men carefully inspecting each other's coat sleeves and collars in quest of lingering hairs, for there was considerable wind in Skagway that summer, and hairs — red, blonde and brunette — were wafted thither and thence by it and were likely to cling to any coat that happened by, and a great deal of trouble was saved by these careful pre-steamer inspections.

As he wandered around the busy town that morning, the Stroller could see that while there was not a legal saloon in the place, for saloons were not legalized in Alaska until the

12

following year, this did not mean that there were no saloons. The Stroller counted at least seventy that morning and probably missed another dozen. Most of the saloons were also money exchanges operating with faro layouts, roulette wheels, blackjack and crap tables and other games sometimes described as games of chance, although in this case the chances were few indeed that the "exchange" would be in any direction but one. Nearly every commodius building that was not a gambling house and saloon was a dancehall, and in some the three were combined, often with a stage thrown in. Business hours for the saloons were around the clock, while the dancehalls usually started at about 4 o'clock in the afternoon and continued until everybody was soused, sometimes twelve and again sixteen hours later, depending on the resisting abilities of the sousees.

It was there and then, as he wandered among the saloons and gambling houses and dancehalls of Skagway, that the Stroller's work of moral uplift suffered a shattering blow and it appeared that his northward journey might have been in vain. From the Everglades of Florida to the shores of Puget Sound the Stroller had sought to elevate the sodden and underdone by persuading them to put a squirt of lemon in it. The shortcomings of this gospel were at once apparent in Skagway — there was no use prescribing for the patient if the prescription could not be filled. And the nation's lemon crop just wasn't up to providing a squirt, even a small one, for all of the drinks then being consumed in Skagway.

But although the Stroller was staggered by this discovery, his natural optimism asserted itself and he determined to continue his missionary work in one way or another and, by precept and example, to lift Skagway from the morass in which she wallowed.

There was one other thing that the Stroller noticed that

morning as he walked around the town. On the sheer rock wall of a mountainside, perhaps a thousand feet above the town and visible from nearly every part of it, someone had painted, in large red letters, the words: "Drink Rocky Mountain Tea." But nobody in Skagway seemed to be paying any heed to that admonition.

SMITH'S ALASKA GUARDS

THE CALENDAR HAD just been turned to the merry month of May in the year 1898 when word reached Skagway that the United States had declared war against Spain. The event itself had happened nearly a week earlier, but those were the days before the submarine telegraph cable was laid northward to Alaska, and the news had to come from Seattle by boat. The news was not wholly unexpected, of course, and ever since the blowing up of the *Maine* in the harbor of Havana nearly three months previously, the red blood of American patriotism had been coursing pell mell through the systems of the residents of the up and coming town of Skagway. And it might be said here that while there were those who would argue about the "coming" part of Skagway, there was no doubt whatever about the "up" part at that time, for a goodly portion of the population was up both day and night. There were some who managed to get a few winks beneath the gaming tables of the Board of Trade, The Bonanza, The Peerless or another of the diverse and sundry resorts, and a few others had homes to which they occasionally repaired and in which they sometimes even slept, but the majority were up at all hours.

But while it was not unexpected, the news that war had actually been declared created a sensation and patriotism began seething, bubbling, fermenting and even boiling. Uncle Sam was in need of fighting men, and that was the only kind of men Skagway had. In fact, it was a dull night indeed when there was not at least one fight on every street corner in town. Fighting men were, in other words, available in droves; all they lacked was organization and guns.

And organization was soon forthcoming, for in no heaving breast in Skagway did patriotism seethe, bubble, ferment and boil more intensely than in that of Jefferson Randolph Smith, more commonly known as Soapy. For several months both Soapy Smith and the Stroller had been conducting services in Skagway and the former had organized everything in sight except the blackjack boosters' union. This, either through oversight or because he realized there was no money in it, he had considerately left to the latter who was, then as always, busily exercising his talent for organizing and promoting causes in which there was no cash return, or at least none upon which he could lay his hands.

Before news of the declaration of war was two hours old in Skagway, Jefferson Randolph Soapy Smith was organizing a military unit, which he called Smith's Alaska Guards, and was circulating a volunteer list. Never was a list or petition more universally or more readily signed. Patriotism had risen to such a pitch that anyone who refused to sign would have been branded a Spanish sympathizer and cast into outer darkness or the Skagway River, whichever was handier at the moment. The names of ministers of the gospel followed those of faro dealers and bartenders on the list, and the Stroller's name was sandwiched between those of the Skylight Kid and Willie the Rat. The list, in addition to setting forth that the signers, individually and collectively, thirsted for enemy blood and yearned to assist in avenging America's honor, served as a petition to the Department of War, asking that it accept the services of Smith's Alaska Guards.

Soapy Smith let it be known that he was an aspirant to the captaincy of the company, but that he desired to be elected by its members in true democratic fashion. Since he was clearly the man of the hour, his election was unanimous and it was agreed that he should name his own official staff, which he did. A tall dignified fellow known as the Senator, whose specialty was a three-card monte game, was made lieutenant. The bouncer at Clancy's was named sergeant, and the head bartender at the Klondike Saloon became chaplain. The Stroller was appointed something or other that had to do with publicity, for Smith's Alaska Guards intended to make history that would merit recording.

Immediately following the organization of the Guards and the naming of a staff, Captain Smith cornered all the ribbon in town for use in making up badges for the members. It did not take him long to do this because Skagway was at that time much longer on overalls and mackinaw suits than it was on ribbon. There was not, in fact, enough ribbon to go around and butcher paper was substituted to fill out. Within a day or two every member had a badge, whether of silk, cotton or paper, with "Smith's Alaska Guards" printed on it in bright red.

After the badges had been distributed, there was a parade which was held in the evening as the days were growing long at that season of the year. It was Skagway's first parade — leaving out the nightly parade from the dance floor to the bar while the caller was wetting his call-box — and it was probably the greatest parade known in Alaska up to that time. It formed up on the waterfront with Captain Soapy Smith to lead it on his white horse. Everyone else marched, or at least they walked, and there was a brass band to set the time and furnish — well, the Stroller was going to say it furnished music, but the band had just been organized by Jake Rice, the proprietor of the People's Theatre, and its member had never had a chance to practice together, so what they furnished may not have been music,

17

but at least it was loud. The band was placed about the middle of the parade so all hands could hear it, and in front of the band and behind it were rank after rank of men, tall men and short men, lean men and fat ones, all moving along as nearly as they could in time to Jake Rice's brass band.

The Stroller would be violating his rule of strict veracity if he were to state that the parade went off without a hitch. At Fifth and Broadway, for some reason, Captain Smith and the head end of the parade turned right while the band and the rear end turned left, but the two parts got together again at Seventh and State and no real harm was done. There was another interruption when the head of the parade got to a place that advertised itself as the Princess Hotel but which was called a number of other things that would not look well in print. Babe Davenport ran out of the place and grabbed Captain Smith's bridle, and was followed by five or six other girls. All were clad in their working uniforms and the Stroller noticed, before he could turn his head away, that what they wore for uniforms was barely visible to the naked eye. The girls demanded that Captain Soapy Smith stop right there and then and organize a Ladies Auxiliary, and while this was going on the rear ranks kept crowding up for a look at the scenery and there was a lot of confusion and a great deal of advice was shouted up to Captain Smith as to what he should do, none of which he took, or at least not right then. Captain Smith finally shooed the girls back inside with something about "Your turn will come later," whatever was meant by that, and the parade got straightened out and started again.

No part of the town was slighted and after about an hour and a half of marching the men were dragging the hay foot and likewise the straw foot and their tongues were hanging out with thirst. Captain Smith decided there had been enough parading for one night and the place where he reached this decision happened to be directly in front of Jeff's Parlors, of which he was the owner. He dismounted from his white horse and one of the men led it away while the captain looked for a good place from which to make a speech. The best and handiest place was the doorway of his saloon, and that is where he stood.

What Captain Smith had to say was very complimentary to his listeners. He said he was proud of them and that he was sure that Smith's Alaska Guards would be ordered to active duty in short order and that this would assure a speedy ending to the war. The Stroller does not remember everything Captain Jefferson Randolph Soapy Smith said in that speech, but he does remember the end of it, which he has always considered a masterpiece.

"You are fine and brave men, each and every one of you," said Captain Smith, "and I am sure that you will unhesitatingly follow me anywhere, and at any time." And with that he turned smartly on his heel and marched into the saloon. He was a born leader of men, was Captain Soapy Smith, and under the circumstances, what could his troops do but follow him? And follow him they did, and it just happened that seven extra bartenders were there, aproned and waiting to start, as they put it, "shoving de booze over de wood."

It was conservatively estimated that Jeff's Parlors took in $2,500 that night, all cash business. Notices on the wall stated plainly and tersely: "No Jaw Bone Goes Here," so only those who had the price or had friends with the price entered into the spirit of the occasion. Moreover, it was only those that had the price or had friends with the price that the "spirit" of the occasion entered into, such as the "spirit" was. The Stroller, in his young and gladsome days, did a little bit of sampling here and there, including white mule in Florida, pine top in Washington State, and on one occasion the contents of Babcock fire extinguishers in then dry Atlanta, Georgia, but never in all of his experience as a sampler did he sample weaker "sacred water" than was served in Jeff's Parlors that night of the big parade — at two-bits a hoist, cash.

When Smith's Alaska Guards finally dispersed that night, it was for the last time. Early the next morning a rumor sped around Skagway that men who had already reached the Klondike were finding six-bits to the pan on every creek, and before noon a thousand men were on the march — not toward Cuba but toward the Summit on their way to Dawson.

But although most of its members could soon have been classed as AWOL, Captain Smith was not yet finished with the Guards. He saw one more opportunity for patriotic endeavor and he was never one to let opportunity slip by without giving it a run for its money. Keeping mum about the fact that the War Department had politely declined the services of Smith's Alaska Guards, the captain announced that a benefit show would be staged to create a fund for the widows and orphans of the members. It was not explained why this was necessary, since few of the members admitted to having either wives or children, but as the cry of "Spanish sympathizer" was still easily raised, nobody asked questions. Patriotism continued at a high level and there was a big advance sale of tickets, some 1,450 of them being exchanged for a dollar each. This assured a full house as the combined seating and standing capacity of the hall where the benefit was staged was only about six hundred.

The show was something of a success so far as entertainment was concerned, and as successes went in Skagway at that time. The Stroller had been badly stung in a Fire Department benefit a few weeks earlier and steered clear of the management and financial end of this one. But as a safeguard against having his patriotism questioned, he

20

did offer to take part in the performance, blacked up his face and sang "I'se a Roving Little Darkey All the Way from Alabam" without getting egged. But the real hit of the show was Claw Finger Kitty and her rendition of "Just Before the Battle, Mother." She pronounced Battle as this it were spelled with an o, and it went over big.

But so far as any widows and orphans were concerned, the show was a dismal failure, for the treasurer disappeared immediately afterward and with him the benefit fund except for $65 or $75 taken in at the door. It was afterward learned that the treasurer was a long-standing acquaintance and associate of Captain Soapy Smith, and it was further learned that the treasurer and Claw Finger Kitty had at one time sacrificed themselves on the alter of conventionality by marrying. Both of them had left, Kitty taking her Bottle song and the treasurer presumably taking $1,450 in coin of the realm.

It was less than two months after the benefit show that Captain Jefferson Randolph Soapy miscalculated just how fast he was on the draw. And when his remains were hurried off to Skagway's small but growing graveyard for the planting ceremonies, fewer than half a dozen of his former troopers joined the procession, and not one of them was wearing the ribbon badge of Smith's Alaska Guards.

BARBARA

THE NEWSPAPER for which the Stroller worked in Skagway during several months in the year 1898 was different in one respect from any other paper with which he has been connected. It had no subscription list and no subscribers, and it sought none. The population of Skagway that year ran anywhere from six thousand to as high as ten thousand, but it was far too transient for a subscription list to be practical or workable. But the paper did have a good many hundreds of patrons who purchased it from salesmen on the street. None of these paper-sellers could be classed as newsboys: they were all men, of all ages and sizes and of assorted previous condition. Many of them found the business of selling papers on the streets and in the stores, saloons, gambling houses, dancehalls and other resorts a remunerative one, but this does not mean that any of them stayed with it very long. They were as foot-loose as their customers, and while the paper had from ten to fifteen paper-sellers, it was seldom the same lot for two successive weeks.

Thus the Stroller was not surprised, one morning about the middle of May, when he was asked to interview an applicant for a job selling papers, but he was surprised when he saw the applicant. It was not a man, but a woman, a little bit of a gray-haired woman with blue eyes and an appealing smile. She gave her age as seventy-six and the same figure would do for her weight, give or take a pound or two. She said her name was Barbara.

The little creature seemed to be a little bit dismayed, and the Stroller talked to her and asked her a number of

22

questions. Where did she come from? Why did she come to Skagway? Did she have a family or any relatives? And did they know she was in Skagway?

Barbara talked quite freely once she was sure she had a sympathetic listener, and it quickly became clear that she had come to Skagway for the same reason thousands of others had come there that year; she wanted to make some money. Barbara was a widow and all of her children were grown and most of them had families of their own. She had been living with one of her married daughters in Butte, Montana, and a few weeks previously she had traveled out to Seattle to visit with an old friend. When the visit was nearing its end, Barbara's daughter had sent her money to return to Butte but instead she bought a ticket to Skagway. No, neither her daughter nor anyone else knew about it. They would have stopped her had they known.

"All my life," she said wistfully, "I've wondered what it would be like to go out among complete strangers and make my own way. I always wanted to try it, and never had the chance. When the chance came, I took it. And here I am!"

And there she was, all seventy-six pounds of her, with her possessions in a worn carpetbag, only a few dollars left in her purse, and the necessity of earning money to live on. Would the Stroller give her a chance to sell papers? Of course he would, and he did, although he had some qualms about it. Privately, the Stroller decided that he would give Barbara a week and then he would write to her daughter in Butte and arrange for her passage home.

But the Stroller need not have worried. Barbara began selling papers and the first money she earned went for a place to live. She paid two dollars for a piano box and made a home of it, a merchant kindly allowing her to locate her home on a vacant strip of ground next to his store. Of course, she took her meals out, but the piano box served as a place to sleep — if Barbara ever slept, which the Stroller sometimes doubted.

It was not long before Barbara was selling more papers and making more money than any dozen paper-sellers in town. The paper, which sold for ten cents a copy, came out in the afternoon around 4 o'clock when everything was working right, and that was just about the time the dancehalls and gambling houses were beginning to get busy. Barbara visited them all — the Board of Trade, the Grotto, and All Nations, Clancy's, The Tivoli, The Balmoral, and all the many others — and she made friends everywhere. Soon the bartenders, faro dealers, case-keepers and even some of the girls, as well as regular customers of the places, were waiting to buy their papers from Barbara rather than from some other seller. Even the boosters and swampers were her friends, although they did not themselves buy papers. Some of the more fastidious of the boosters would spread a newspaper on the sawdust under a crap table before crawling in for the night, but an old paper served as well as a fresh one for that purpose.

Barbara had one sales method that was all her own, and the Stroller happened to see it demonstrated one afternoon in Jimmy Ryan's Nugget Saloon, a place much frequented by the packers and muleskinners who were hauling freight up the trail and by the construction men who were then starting to build the White Pass Railroad. A big rawboned fellow had just lost seven straight times on the black and was giving vent to his feelings. He cursed the game, the dealer, the country, the climate and several other things that came to his mind, and it was plain to see that he was no green hand at the business of expressing himself. As this molten flow poured forth, Barbara entered the place and walked directly to the fellow. She stopped in front of him, turned those blue eyes up to his face and with that appealing smile, she asked, "Would you like to buy a paper, mister?"

24

The cursing stopped abruptly and the fellow stood there with his mouth wide open. His face turned red. Then he shut his mouth and thrust a hairy paw into a pocket. He pulled out a silver dollar, thrust it at Barbara with a muttered, "Keep the change," grabbed a paper and buried his face in it as though it were the most interesting thing he had ever run across. Barbara thanked him with another smile and went on to the next customer.

Barbara also met all the steamers from the south, and there was a great many of them that summer, sometimes three or four in a single day, each loaded to capacity with eager gold-seekers — and "capacity" was a very elastic term on the steamers. While the people who were then in Skagway eagerly awaited the steamers or papers and news from "down below," the arriving passengers were equally eager for news of Skagway and the Klondike gold fields and about conditions on the trail and the river. The sale of papers became brisk as soon as the gang plank was in place, and here, again, Barbara quickly made friends. The officers and crews on the boats soon got to know her and they passed the word to their passengers: "Be sure to get your paper from the little old lady."

By the time Barbara had been selling papers for a month, she was known to nearly everybody in Skagway and her business was improving all the time. The printer's devil, who took the papers from the press, folded them and stacked them for the sellers, was soon making two stacks — one for the men sellers and the other, equally high, for Barbara. And on more than one occasion Barbara sold all of her stack and dipped into that of the men. She made the Stroller her banker, so he knew just how much she was taking in. All of her earnings except the cost of three meals a day were turned over to him, and what he was saving for Barbara was several times more than he could manage to save for himself.

Then one day in August, Barbara came to the Stroller with tears in her eyes and sorrow in her voice. An old reprobate had proposed to her that she leave her piano box and move into his cabin. He had not only proposed this, but insisted that she do so, and he was bothering her constantly. She pointed out the man and the Stroller interviewed him and explained that if he was still in Skagway after the next steamer sailed for Seattle, "the gang" would be informed of his activities. The Stroller went even stronger. He told the old cuss to pack his kit and camp on the end of the dock until the steamer sailed. The warning was heeded, and Barbara had no further trouble.

The Stroller now confesses that he was bluffing just a little when he threatened to tell "the gang." There was, by that time, no organized "gang" in Skagway. Soapy Smith had been eliminated from the scene early in July and the members of his gang who had not taken to the woods or been put in jail were making themselves very inconspicuous. But the Stroller felt sure that there were few men in Skagway, good, bad or in between, who would not have turned out to help chastise a brute who would molest the little old lady who sold papers, and the chastisement would undoubtedly have been far more severe than the sentence imposed by the Stroller.

As the days grew short and the snowline moved down the mountains, the Stroller began to have misgivings about Barbara's wintering in Skagway. At that time he had not yet spent a winter there himself and he imagined an Alaska winter would be much worse than it is. So one day he had a talk with her and suggested that she could well afford a trip back home and that she had earned a vacation. Moreover, he told her, selling papers during the winter would not be nearly so lucrative as during the busy months of summer. Fortunately, Barbara fell in with this idea and the Stroller made an accounting of her money. She had

$1,350, which she had saved in just five months. Of this total, $1,200 was exchanged for a bank draft which was mailed to her daughter in Butte. A ticket was purchased to Seattle, and she had something over $100 left for her fare from Seattle to Butte and for incidental expenses.

Three or four weeks later a letter arrived from Barbara's daughter, saying that Barbara had arrived safely home and expressing appreciation for the treatment she had received. Later on, Barbara wrote to inquire whether her job would be open in the spring and to request that her piano box home not be disturbed as she hoped to return.

And that was the last time the Stroller ever heard of Barbara. The Stroller went on to Dawson and would not have been in Skagway had she returned there, but she never returned. The site where she had her home in the piano box is almost directly opposite the present Golden North Hotel, and the box was still there several years later when the Stroller passed through Skagway, although it has since disappeared.

This is not much of a story, but it goes to show that a nice little old lady was safe in Skagway at a time when it was being called the toughest town on earth, and was doing what it could to maintain that reputation. She was as safe there as she would have been in any staid, elm-shaded old eastern town where they blow out the candles and go to bed at 9 o'clock every night of the week.

A
FACE
LIKE A
BULL PUP

IT ALL STARTED when Ham Grease Jimmy, in a contemplative frame of mind, announced to the Burn-'Em-Up Kid in his usual forthright manner that "dis moll which Paddy de Pig is stuck on has got a face on her like a bull pup."

The Burn-'Em-Up Kid may have many faults, as has sometimes been alleged by those who know him, but selfishness is not one of them and he has never been known to hoard a good thing when he got onto it. Consequently it was no time at all before Ham Grease Jimmy's remark was making the rounds and not much longer before it reached the ears of Paddy the Pig. Considering that the remark reflected on his taste in matters concerning the opposite sex, Paddy the Pig deeply resented the imputation and lost no time in taking steps to vindicate his honor and his judgment.

But as Paddy the Pig did not place much reliance in anything told by the Burn-'Em-Up Kid, he decided to hold a conversation with Ham Grease Jimmy to learn at first hand whether the latter had actually made the remark. Ham Grease had made it and he was ready and willing to stand by it. "If youse tink youse can make me take back what I said about de jane, youse can open up wid de hostilities any time, an' de sooner de better, see?" said Ham Grease Jimmy.

Paddy the Pig saw, but he hesitated to open hostilities, and for good reason. The reason was that Ham Grease Jimmy had a job boosting for the blackjack game at the Wheel of Fortune gambling house and had been eating regularly for as much as two weeks. As a result he was in much better shape than Paddy the Pig who had been eating only now and then when the lady referred to as "de moll" slipped him the price, the lady being Big Bo Peep who was employed at the Dainty Toe Dance Hall. Paddy, in other words, lacked confidence in his physical prowess when it was stacked up against the prowess of Ham Grease Jimmy.

There was at that time, which was early in 1898, a natural-born arbiter in Skagway, and to him all disputes not settled on the spot by blows or weapons were eventually taken. The name of this arbiter was Jefferson Randolph Smith, but he was generally known as Soapy when he was not referred to as Captain, as he invariably was by the numerous "Kid" element of the town, and while Soapy Smith's usual arbitering concerned three shells and a small but lively pea, he was willing to take on other matters upon occasion.It was to him that Paddy the Pig carried his grievance against Ham Grease Jimmy, complaining that the object of the slur, Big Bo Peep was in fact a lady at all times, drunk as well as sober.

Now Captain Soapy Smith was nothing if not diplomatic when the occasion required, and when Paddy presented his case, Soapy at once recognized that this was a matter in which diplomacy of the highest grade was essential. The reason for this was that both Paddy the Pig and Ham Grease Jimmy had many friends in the town of Skagway, and these friends had been taking sides in the dispute until much of the population was entered on one side or the other. This extended all the way up from the boosters, which included both Paddy the Pig and Ham Grease Jimmy when they were working, through the swampers, bouncers, dance-callers, case-keepers and lookouts to the very elite of Skagway's highest and inner circle of society, such as faro dealers and bartenders who could be trusted not to steal more than half the cash intake during their shifts. All of these people were being urged by Ham Grease Jimmy or by Paddy the Pig to step over to the Dainty Toe Dance Hall and see for themselves whether Big Bo Peep did or did not have a face on her like a bull pup.

Captain Soapy Smith, knowing that others had been taking sides in the matter and being, as previously stated, diplomatic, discreetly sidestepped the responsibility of deciding the question. After some pondering of the issue involved, however, he did agree to act as chairman in the case provided that a sort of jury composed of half a dozen disinterested parties, could be selected to hear the evidence, inspect "de moll," adjudicate the matter and decide whether Ham Grease Jimmy was or was not justified in making the statement attributed to him and which he did not deny.

Both men agreed to this recommendation, but another snag was encountered when each of the litigants claimed the privilege of selecting at least two-thirds of the men tried and true, women having been ruled out from the start as being prejudiced in the first place and unauthorized by law to sit on juries in Alaska, anyway. But Soapy poured the oil and removed the snag by offering to select the jury himself, and this was agreed to when he promised to pick the most substantial and upstanding citizens of Skagway to serve.

The Stroller is proud to say that he was the first one to be selected by Captain Smith; not that he considers that he has ever been substantial as he understands that term, but that he has ever and anon been upstanding through the hours of daylight and a good part of the night as well. Five others were persuaded to serve with the Stroller and the committee held several meetings but failed to reach a decision. The Stroller was sworn to secrecy regarding the deliberations of the body, and while many years have since rolled away, some of the interested parties are still around. He will only say, therefore, that after a visit to the Dainty Toe Dance Hall and a consideration of the evidence in the case, the jury was hopelessly deadlocked. Two of the members felt that the girl had been slandered by Ham Grease Jimmy; two of them claimed that he had described her countenance precisely, and the other two brought in a lengthy report in which they asserted that they would not subject a bull pup to such a comparison and offered a number of substitute descriptions for Big Bo Peep.

The chairman, exercising his diplomacy, refused to cast a ballot, declaring that it could not break the deadlock since no majority vote would result. He did suggest that he be empowered as chairman to report progress now and then when either the the litigants became impatient, and was duly authorized to do so. Things drifted along in that manner for a couple of months and until that fateful July day when Captain Jefferson Randolph Soapy Smith's system proved unequal to digesting a .45 calibre bullet. With his demise the six arbiters were automatically discharged; at least they took advantage of the occasion and discharged themselves with thanks.

Two weeks later the Stroller, in quest of a printer who had wandered from the path of sobriety, entered the Always Open Gambling House — No Color Line, and there embraced in each other's arms and sound asleep under a crap table were Paddy the Pig and Ham Grease Jimmy. That same afternoon Paddy called on the Stroller and said:

"Youse fellers might just as well forget about dat investigation. De moll pulled out dis mornin' for Seattle wid de Klondike Kid. He blew in from Dawson last night wid a poke full of brass filings which he told her was gold dust. She fell for it an' agreed to pay his fare to Seattle where he could sell de dust for $5000 an' den dey would get married and visit his ancestral estates in de sout' of France. Dat was de guff he give her, an' she fell for it an' dey was on de *Dolphin* when it left dis mornin'. Just betwixt ourselves, you an' me, Ham Grease hit de nail right smack on de head wid dat story 'bout de jane havin' a mug like a bull pup an' I don't hold no grudge against him. In fact," said Paddy the Pig, "I ain't so sure but what Ham Grease was payin' de jane a compliment when he said it."

THE
PACK TRAIN
RESTAURANT

IT WAS IN THE early fall of 1897 that Anton Stanish and Louis Ceovich wrestled their restaurant outfit ashore on a beach at the head of Lynn Canal. That was where the new town of Skagway was budding into life as a second gateway to the Klondike and a rival to the older town of Dyea, a few miles away. Buildings were at that time very scarce in Skagway and Tony and Louie, as the two were known, secured a large tent, set up their outfit and began dispensing "ham and."

That was before the White Pass Railroad had been built or even started, and pack trains of horses, mules and burros were much in evidence in the new town. They were used to transport mining outfits and supplies from tidewater over the White Pass Trail to Lake Bennett at the headwaters of the Yukon River where they were loaded on boats or barges to continue their journey to the Klondike. So Tony and Louie named their place of business the Pack Train and began making history. There were dozens of other restaurants in Skagway in those early days, but most of them were of a transitory nature and many of them changed owners oftener than the coffee grounds were emptied. But the Pack Train remained, thrived and became a fixture and a landmark.

If Tony and Louie ever slept during the first two years after they opened the Pack Train, they were never caught at it. Big Louie was the cook and he hovered over the range which was four feet one way and twelve the other, while little Tony darted back and forth behind the counter as though strung on a wire. And ever and anon Tony's shrill falsetto voice would carry back to Louie with "Eint da ham and." Between the hours of 1 a.m. and 6 a.m., when business slacked off a little, Tony and Louie took turns resting and peeling potatoes for the next day, but the Pack Train never closed and you could get a meal at any hour. And it was such a meal as gave the place a reputation from Peru to Point Barrow. A steak served at the Pack Train always seemed more tender than those obtained elsewhere, while the canned oysters were somehow made to taste as though they had left Chesapeake Bay the day before.

The business was moved, after a few months, from the tent in which it was first opened to a modest building, where it remained for more than a dozen years. It shared this building with the Pack Train Saloon, but Tony and Louie had no interest in the saloon and a partition separated the two. There was, however, a connecting door so that if a patron of the restaurant wanted "something" with his meal it could be secured from next door, whether it was Budweiser at five cents a scoop or Mumm's at $10 a quart. And not infrequently Louie called upon the resources of the saloon to provide the wherewithall to fill an order, such as salmon bellies stewed in champagne or eggs sizzled in beer, for there was no telling what a customer might order after a grueling pack trip to the Summit, a big winning in one of the gambling houses, or a hard night on the dance floor.

What might be termed the nighthawk branch of Skagway society, which included a very large portion of the total population at that time, was divided into many different levels. Boosters for the blackjack games and swampers in the saloons were at the lowest level, but there was caste even among them. Those engaged at the Board of Trade and the Peerless considered themselves above those employed at the Red Onion or the Grotto, while the latter looked down on those working at the Hungry Pup or the Home of Hootch. A cut above the boosters and swampers were the lookouts and bouncers, with the dance-callers and case-keepers a step higher. Faro dealers were generally considered to be at the top of this heap, but bartenders were rated at several different levels, depending on whether they were high-class, low-class or in between. These distinctions were a little difficult to understand and are even harder to explain, and the Stroller can perhaps best illustrate with an example. The Stroller recollects an instance when a bartender went on shift at 7:30 p.m., at which time there was change in the cash drawer to the amount of $12.50. Business was brisk and the poor fellow was leg weary and wan when he went off duty at 7:30 the following morning. The assets in the till then amounted to $7.50. Now, that fellow was what was considered a middle-class bartender. Had he been a high-class practitioner the total would have been $12.50 or maybe a little bit more, while if he had been at the lowest end of the scale, the drawer would have been empty.

But none of these distinctions, nor any others, were recognized at the Pack Train. There all met on a common level and caste was unknown. All money looked alike to Tony and Louie, and all who had the price were welcome as well as many who were, temporarily or permanently, on jawbone. The swamper at the Mangy Dog Saloon got just as good treatment and as much for his money at the Pack Train as did the wife of the district judge or the faro dealer at Lee Guthrie's, and between the hours of 6 a.m. and midnight few of the seats were long vacant. Many a time at the Pack Train the Stroller began to blow his soup while seated between a pastor from the Union Church and the dance-caller at Clancy's Music Hall. And by the time he was ready for the prune pie, the preacher's seat wold have been taken by Sweet Geraldine who, when sufficiently sober, did a hoochy-coochy turn at Dave Blake's Palace of Delight, while on the other side the fellow who admonished the boys to "corral your heifers for the next turn" would have retired in favor of a YMCA secretary, the bouncer at the Balmoral, or perhaps Captain Soapy Smith himself. And in the latter event, Captain Smith would usually insist upon paying for all three meals, for whatever else might have been said about him he was a liberal and generous spender and when his supply ran low he would sally forth and replenish his exchequer by methods peculiar to himself.

As Skagway advanced to the tablecloth and napkin stage and wives began arriving to join their husbands, private boxes were added in the Pack Train and tablecloths appeared on the tables. Also, the door leading to the saloon was sometimes closed or partly closed. The language that oozed through it when open was not always exactly what wives had been accustomed to "back yonder." But during the next dozen years or so, table linen and private boxes were the only innovations, and the masses flocked there to eat. Finger-bowl joints opened every now and then with great eclat and endeavored to wrest the trade from the Pack Train, but the grocer and butcher usually closed them out at the end of the first month.

The man who had but ten minutes for a meal went to the Pack Train, where he received prompt attention. So did the businessman who wished to blow himself for a dinner for an important customer. And the married man who was in the wrong and wished to placate his wife invariably took her to the Pack Train and ordered unjointed fried chicken with thick gravy and French fries. This meal would be served within thirty minutes after the order was placed and the placating would be so successful that like as not friend wife was reaching across the table for hubby's hand by the time the dessert and coffee showed up. As a placator of offended wives, the Pack Train was equal to a jewelry store and better than a couple of tickets for Ladies' Night at the People's Theater.

Travelers who were going to the Interior for the first time in those days often imagined that they would get nothing but bacon and beans to eat after leaving Skagway and they gorged themselves with "one more square" at the Pack Train. And, on the other hand, people who were coming out from the Interior always looked forward to and talked about the fine big feed they would enjoy at the Pack Train after they reached Skagway and they were not disappointed. The Pack Train got them going and coming and it prospered mightily.

But times changed in Skagway as they do everywhere and there came a day when the business center of the town had shifted until the Pack Train was away out on the edge of things, almost out of town. Tony and Louie took stock of the changing conditions and Louie was for quitting entirely. But Tony wanted to hang on, so he purchased Louie's interest and the latter laid aside the white cap and cook's apron he had worn with distinction for fifteen years. Tony closed up the old stand and followed the crowd to where it had located, a few blocks to the south. But for some reason the halo which had for so many years hovered over the old Pack Train never settled over the new. Tony tried it for a couple of years, during which he was both cook and waiter. Then he gave up and locked the front door, bid a fond and lingering good-bye to Skagway and, with money bulging from every pocket, headed south. He settled in Oregon and started a hog and hen ranch so he could continue, his friends used to say, to handle the "ham and."

But the lure of the North had permeated Tony, and after

a year or so of grubbing stumps, hunting hens' nests and slopping pigs, he sold the ranch and journeyed back. This time he stopped in Ketchikan where he opened a restaurant. He did not call it the Pack Train — Ketchikan is not and never has been a pack train town — but his new place has been very successful.

The Stroller has often thought of the motley crowd that used to mount the stools in front of the bare counter of the old Pack Train to bark at a stack of hots or guzzle soup — the boosters and bartenders, the gamblers and businessmen, the mule-skinners, the queens of the dancehalls and all the others who lighted in Skagway so long ago, tarried briefly and went on their respective ways. All of them rubbed elbows at the Pack Train and met there on common ground. Just as there was but one Chilkoot Pass, one Whitehorse Rapids and one Klondike, so there was but one Pack Train Restaurant, one Tony and one Louie. And in their day the latter three constituted the most popular trinity, aside from straight whiskey, water and then more whiskey, ever known in the North.

MEMORIAL DAY
1898

MEMORIAL DAY in the year 1898 was a very special occasion in the new but busy town of Skagway, since no function of a patriotic nature had ever been held there and this was to be the town's first observance of this holiday. In previous years the only white inhabitants of the place had been a few squaw men and the only days they observed or remembered were those on which their squaws brought home king salmon. But by May, 1898, the Star of Empire had taken its way northward until between six and eight thousand people were mingling with the sands at the head of Lynn Canal. So, as May 30 approached, it was decided to celebrate the day in a manner befitting the solemnity of the occasion. The Stroller, always the goat, was named chairman of the committee to make the necessary arrangements, including the selection of a speaker.

It was first proposed that there be a parade, but when it was recalled that Skagway's first parade, on the occasion of the organization of Smith's Alaska Guards, had ended up in Soapy Smith's saloon and that nobody got home before daylight, if they got home at all, this idea was vetoed and it was decided to have the exercises indoors. As a result there was a good deal of rivalry for the privilege of supplying a hall for the program and several places were offered free of charge if the bar could be kept open during the program. But the committee decided against this, too, and selected the most commodious place in town. This was the Comique Concert Hall, about which columns might be written, although they would not be suitable for bedtime stories. It was not conducted for those who went to bed. Owned at that time by Jap Tommy, who got his walking papers from the people of Skagway a few weeks later during the Soapy Smith riot, the Comique was a combined gambling house, saloon, dancehall, theater and the Stroller wots not what else. (He has an idea, but won't mention it here; far be it for the Stroller to give that emporium of evil a worse reputation than was visible to the naked eye.) But the place did have a stage and a large seating capacity, and those were what the committee was after.

It so happened that about that time there arrived in Skagway from the grasshopper-ridden state of Kansas an aged lawyer, intent on starting anew in the northern town and anxious for an opportunity to present himself before the people among whom he had decided to cast his lot. He boldly requested the Stroller to give him a place on the Memorial Day program. The Stroller acceded to the request and has been a changed man ever since.

Came finally the day and the hour. The hall was packed and it is not probable that a similar crowd was ever assembled on the American continent, for the word "motley" is without meaning when a description of that bunch is attempted. On the first three rows of benches were seated ninety-three widows, of whom less than half a dozen were of the variety known as "sod." The husbands of the eight-seven others were roaming somewhere on the face of the earth with cans tied to them.

The services opened with a prayer, the first and only one ever heard in the Comique. That was followed by a number from the band — five cornets and an equal number of slide trombones fighting it out to see which could reach the high note first. There were some songs by the audience

— the widows could all warble like meadow larks — and then the Stroller introduced the battle scarred Kansan and stated that the old soldier, who was a member of the Grand Army of the Republic, would make a short talk.

At the end of two hours that hero of a thousand battles, real and imaginary, was still going strong. After winning at Gettysburg, Antietam, the Wilderness, Lookout Mountain and Missionary Ridge and explaining in detail how he had baptized virgin soil with rebel blood, he marched from Atlanta to the sea and returned in time to take part in the siege of Richmond. There he out-generaled General Grant, but by the time he was well along on his third hour the Confederate capital had not yet fallen.

The old warrior drank four gallons of ice water and every now and then he handed the Stroller, who was squirming in a chair near the speaker's table, a handkerchief to wring out and return. Every time the speaker stopped for a glass of ice water, half a dozen of the audience made a break for the door, and once when the water pitcher was replenished a note was passed up to the Stroller with the message: "Kill him, or we will kill you!"

Those who escaped from the hall gathered outside where a council of war was held, as the Stroller learned later. Several proposals were submitted, but it was finally concluded that while the old soldier had suffered enough during the war, the Stroller should be strung up for inflicting upon the populace such an inexhaustible, self-lubricating, perpetual motion speaker. It was fortunate for the Stroller that he happened to owe the Blackjack Kid ten dollars just then and that the latter overheard the plan. And since the Blackjack Kid did not wish to see the Stroller disposed of until the debt had been settled, he slipped in through the stage door and hissed: "Dey ain't set no watch on de back door yet. Get out while you can." The Stroller got.

41

It was five days later that the Stroller silently stole down out of the mountains, sneaked into the Pack Train Restaurant and ordered ham and eggs for four, to be followed by three full stacks of hots. If he was going to be hanged, he did not propose to go through with it on an empty stomach. Luckily for the Stroller, however, the attention of the public had been removed from him and was centered right then on the Evaporated Kid, who had been caught in the act of entering the room of Little Egypt through the key hole while she was doing her celebrated contortion act at Frank Clancy's Music Hall and Club Rooms.

Before another Memorial Day came around the Comique Music Hall had burned down and the Stroller has always suspected that the fire was of incendiary origin, the people of Skagway not caring to take another chance. As for the Stroller, although he was tolerated during the remainder of his stay in Skagway, he was never fully reinstated in the estimate of the public and to this day there are old-timers there who whisper, "I pity his family." And the Stroller has never since ventured within the city limits of Skagway on a Memorial Day. It is not that he believes his life is longer in danger but that he shudders at the memory of how close he came to being Alaska's only fatality of the Civil War.

THE BLACKJACK BOOSTERS' UNION

WHERE IS THE blackjack booster of yesteryear?

He has went.

His once familiar haunts will know him no more forever.

It was in Skagway in the glorious year of 1898 that the Stroller, in his efforts to uplift the sodden and underdone and interest them in higher and nobler things, or at least to put a squirt of lemon in it, helped the blackjack boosters to organize their union and get it on its feet. There were at that time at least twenty-five blackjack games running in Skagway, and as each game worked two shifts of boosters of four men each, there were something like 200 potential union members of whom upward of 190 would stand to attention when the call, "Hey there, Kid" was heard. And the boosters did not by any means include all of the "Kid" element in Skagway, which numbered in the hundreds.

But for every "Kid" in Skagway there was a smooth individual who toiled not, neither did he spin — except yarns framed for the purpose of protecting himself. If a hold-up was committed, a drunk rolled, or a money drawer tapped, it was always a "Kid" who was the goat, although in nine cases out of ten the beneficiary of the job was a member of the gentry who could afford to patronize a laundry and who fared sumptuously every day of the week. But a "Kid" could be convicted any and every time

43

that injured society decided a conviction necessary.

From his hut by the side of the road — and not wholly figuratively speaking — the Stroller has watched the race of men go by, good, bad and indifferent, and from his observation it is the latter class that most needs but has the fewest friends. Certainly the blackjack boosters as the Stroller knew them in Skagway belonged to the class with few friends.

It was wholly by accident, however, that the Stroller got an insight into the private lives of the boosters and began to take an interest in their welfare. A tramp printer had wandered from the fold and it was while in search of him that the Stroller visited the Blaze of Glory gambling house about 9 o'clock that Monday morning. Prior to that time he had given little thought to the boosters, imagining in his ignorance that they slept in beds, ate three meals a day and otherwise lived as human beings. But that visit to the Blaze of Glory enlightened him and it was then that he learned that the blackjack booster lived close to his business — so close that he slept under the gaming table and washed his face at the sink behind the bar, when he washed it at all.

There had been a strenuous session the previous night. As a rule the gambling houses closed down about 4 o'clock in the morning, but a steamer had arrived from Seattle late Sunday afternoon bringing a fresh bunch of rubes from the Alfalfa Belt, and all the games in town had worked full blast until the "pickins" began to play out in the grey light of early dawn. The quartet of boosters at the Blaze of Glory had then sought rest for their weary limbs beneath the gaming board, but scarcely had they fallen asleep when the swamper came along and swept them out from under the table. It happened to be the one day in the month when he changed the sawdust on the floor. Still yearning for sleep, the boosters then occupied four chairs

44

at the table and hoisted their feet upon it. There they were when the Stroller arrived, with their heads hanging over the backs of the chairs and their mouths wide open, deeply engaged in wooing Nature's sweet restorer.

It was when the Stroller looked at those four pair of feet on the table that he realized that blackjack boosting was a calling that required elevating. Of the eight feet on that table, six were looking the world in the face, sans soles of shoes and soles of socks. The uppers of the shoes were partly intact, but the soles had tendered their resignations and so far as getting back to Nature was concerned, the wearers of those shoes were in close contact with the old dame.

Realizing the futility of attempting reform work as an outsider that night the Stroller applied for and secured a job as booster for the blackjack game at the All Nations.One shift was sufficient to identify him as a booster, and the second night he called a strike. It happened to be low tide and the strike meeting was held under the Pacific Coast Steamship Company dock. The surroundings were somewhat sordid, but so was the crowd that assembled. Everyone except the Stroller was armed with a sandbag, a club or some other kind of weapon. They had been jobbed so often that they could not believe anything but deceit was in store for them.

The Stroller took the chair, the "chair" being a slippery boulder embedded in the mud, and quickly explained the object of the meeting and the benefits that would accrue from organizing their strength. As the cold and slimy beach under the dock was bad for shoes and worse for the feet they more or less contained, no time was wasted in oratory. The Granulated Kid made a motion that a committee on resolutions be appointed. It was quickly seconded by the Down and Out Kid, there were loud calls for the question and the motion prevailed. The chair appointed the Burn-Em-Up Kid, Four Finger Joe and the Evaporated Kid to the committee and at that point the Nanny Goat Kid, his teeth rattling from the cold, injected, "I moves we hunt a fire." There was no need to put the question; at the mention of a fire the meeting broke up.

The tide was unfavorable when time came for the next meeting and it was held in a dog corral behind the Fifth Avenue Hotel. The following resolution was there presented by the committee:

"Whereas, us is humans an' entitled to de consideration due to humans; and

"Whereas, de dealers an' case-keepers an' others connected wid de games treats us like we is de dust of de earth an' ain't got no feelin's nor nothin'; an'

"Whereas, us denounces as inimical to de moral atmosphere of de place de manner of life of many of dese dealers an' lookouts, especially de ginks dat has wives and' children on de outside. Now, therefore, be it

"Resolved, dat de worm has turned round; an' be it further

"Resolved, dat while we is still willin' to boost for our board an' to continue sleepin' under de tables, we demands dat we be fed three times a day instead of twice as heretofore; an' in dis connection we emphasizes de point dat we is entitled to at least one solid meal per day. De other two may continue to be soup such as we is used to, but de one square is to cost no less than twenty-five cents, and furthermore, we is to be allowed to order whipped cream twice each week for anything we wants to use it on, whether it is prune pie or salmon bellies; an' be it further

"Resolved, dat we get de addresses of de families of dese high-flyin' dealers and others of our superiors, most of which never belonged to de gamblin perfeshon until dey landed here, an' dat we swipe a collection of de pictures of de skirts dese ginks is runnin' around wid, to send back to de homes of our oppressors in de event dey don't come to time; an' finally, be it

"Resolved, dat de name of dis organization is de Amalgamated Order of Blackjack Boosters and dat us members binds ourselves to observe de terms of dis resolution; an' any booster caught scabbin' for two soups per day or otherwise violatin' de rules is to be torn asunder an' de pieces scattered to de four winds."

As the wind only blows north and south in Skagway, this was amended to read "two winds," and with that amendment the resolution was unanimously adopted. The Skylight Kid was elected president and the Two-Bit Kid was named scribe. No treasurer was elected as the members did not have any finances and did not contemplate acquiring any.

The managers, dealers, lookouts, case-keepers and others of the fraternity were not at first inclined to take seriously the stand of the boosters. Then, within a week, more than 200 pictures disappeared from mantels, dressers, walls and other places where they were kept, and mystery stalked rampant. Copies of that portion of the resolution which discussed the disposal of these pictures were then struck off and scattered around in proximity to the gaming tables, and there was an immediate change. The sawdust under the tables was changed twice a week instead of once a month; three meals a day became the custom, and whipped cream was frequently on the menu when boosters dined. Thereafter and as long as there was any demand for boosters, the calling was looked up to and respected.

When Skagway began to miss on some of her cylinders, the "Kid" element moved to the Interior where it flourished for a few years and until the lawmakers in Ottawa said of gambling, in no uncertain terms: "Thou Shalt Not." Then the "Kid" element disappeared, and where it went, the Stroller never knew. He has lines on thousands of old-

47

timers of the North, but they do not include any of the "Kids" who joined the Amalgamated Order of Blackjack Boosters there under the Pacific Coast Steamship Company dock at Skagway. If any member is still living and will write to the Stroller, the latter will send him a faro marker. It was received by the Stroller from a leading and influential gambler to indicate that he owed the Stroller $25, which he still owes.

NO
JAWBONE
HERE

NEARLY ALL business in the new and busy town of Skagway was being done on a cash basis when the Stroller landed there in the early spring of 1898, and both then and for a considerable time afterward the "No Jawbone Here" signs were prominently displayed. If you wanted a bunk for the night, you paid for it before you had your sleep, not afterward. Bartenders didn't even reach for the bottle until they saw the color of the customer's money, and in the dancehalls the ivory chip which entitled you to a waltz or a two-step with the heifer of your choice had to be purchased before the music started. Now and then Tony and Louie at the Pack Train Restaurant would allow one of their steady customers to stand them off for a meal or two if things had been running against him, but this was a rarity rather than a rule.

All of this was made necessary by the highly transient nature of Skagway's population during its first few years, when thousands of people were merely passing through and hundreds of others had stopped off only long enough to round up a stake that would carry them on to the Klondike. And there were many in both classes who, if they had ever owned a sense of financial responsibility, had left it behind when they kissed their wives, children and other kinfolk good-bye and headed north.

And in Skagway the "no credit" rule applied not only to individuals but to most of the business establishments,

49

many of these being almost as transient as their customers. Restaurants, saloons, fruit stands, cigar stores, meat markets and dozens of other assorted emporiums opened in tents or shanties, flourished for a day, a week or a month and then disappeared. There were also, of course, a good many substantial mercantile firms, but they became substantial by keeping their ledger sheets clean and any that had allowed extensive credit to run up on its books would soon have been left with the books and little else to show for its enterprise.

By the early months of 1898 Skagway had an electric light plant, and even electricity was sold, as nearly as could be, for cash. Established and reputable business houses would have been allowed to settle their bills for electricity at the end of the month, but few of them had such bills. They were conservative and they stuck to kerosene lamps and tallow candles. Electric lights were expensive — thirty-five cents per night for each 16-candlepower globe — but in spite of this they were greatly favored by the saloons and dancehalls where business was thought to be attracted in proportion to the brilliance of the illumination.But such places, if they did not pay each day for the electricity used the night before, found themselves in darkness when the curtains of another night were pinned down.

The Stroller never saw this fact more clearly demonstrated than one afternoon about 4:30 when he called at the Savoy Saloon and Dancehall to deliver an order of printing, a batch of lottery tickets, and of course to collect for the same. Dancing usually began at the Savoy at 4 o'clock, but on this day the joint was dark except for the yellow and sputtering rays of two candles, one at each end of the long bar, and the whole place was pervaded with an atmosphere of gloom. Back of the bar, silent and scowling, stood the two proprietors of the place and as the Stroller peered at them in the dim light of the tallow dips, he realized that it was not an auspicious time for the collection of a bill. So he backed up against the wall and waited to see what would happen.

As his eyes became accustomed to the dimness of the interior, the Stroller could see that the members of the orchestra were on their platform with their instruments in readiness, although no sound came forth. The floor manager was lit to the eyes and in fine fettle, but he too was unusually silent. Some of the "attractions" of the place, including Gum Boots Kitty, the Pink 'Un, Big Bess and Guzzling Gertie, were standing around chewing gum and muttering curses. And up in the muslin ceiling was the big hole where the electrician who installed the wiring had dropped through and landed in the middle of the blackjack table, an event which had nearly broken up the game to say nothing of the electrician. The Stroller also noticed that a man with a pair of wire pliers in his hand was backed up against the opposite wall and he recognized him as an electrician for the light company, although not the same one who had installed the wiring.

There was not long to wait. The Chills and Fever Kid, breathless from running, stumbled through the door and gasped: "Hey, dere, youse wid de nippers. Turn on de juice. Here's de receipted bill from last night."

Two minutes later the electrician, who had disconnected the circuit and was camped there awaiting this development, had performed his duty. The electric rays flashed through the den of iniquity, the orchestra burst forth with the inspiring strains of "Buffalo Gals," and the argonauts in hobnail shoes, gum boots and mocassins heeded the call of the floor manager to "Grab yo honeys." The dance was on and joy was unconfined. The Stroller delivered his work, collected his bill, had a tinroof — it was on the house — and returned to his own emporium.

The crisis at the Savoy was ended, at least until its light bill fell due again the next day.

But in Skagway as elsewhere, the Stroller followed his custom of sometimes saying "yes" when he should have said "no" and thus failed to keep his ledger sheets as unsullied as those of the substantial business men, which may be one of the reasons he never became substantial. When he came to leave Skagway for Dawson, late in the year 1898, the Stroller could locate only two or three of the several dozen people who had accounts on his books, and he collected from only one of them. Nor has he located any of the others since that time, and gradually the old accounts have been scratched off as uncollectible until today only one remains. The Stroller has tried on several occasions to collect this one last account and still has hopes of doing so, although with each passing year the hope grows dimmer. This is the account:

```
Dr.  Finance Community
     Fourth of July Celebration, 1898
     Skagway, Alaska
     500 posters, two color .............................................$50.00
     2000 handbills .................................................. 12.00
     2500 Badges, Paper...................................... 17.50
       1 Greased Pole ......................................... 5.00
                                                             _____
                                                              $84.50
```

And this is the way it all came about:

When Skagway's first Fourth of July approached, a mass meeting was called to make plans for the celebration and a large number of committees were appointed. There was a Finance Committee to collect funds for the various expenses, which included prizes, decorations, printing, an orchestra for the dance, and so forth. There was a Fireworks Committee, a Parade Committee, a Dance

Committee and a committee for each one of the sports events. The Stroller and Jefferson Randolph Smith, commonly known as Soapy, were named co-chairmen of the Greased Pole Committee, and this appointment suited the Stroller in every way. He did not see where there could be much work connected with it, and he assumed that Soapy would look after what little there was. Apparently Soapy assumed the same thing about the Stroller, and he was the better assumer, for when nothing had been done by the afternoon of July 3, the Stroller got cold feet and hired a man to cut a suitable pole in the woods, trim it, smooth it, grease it and set it up in the designated spot. For these labors he paid the man $5 which he proposed to collect, along with the printing bill, when the Finance Committee settled up after the celebration was over.

The Fourth of July dawned fair and bright and the celebration came off without more than a normal amount of confusion. Anvils and shotguns were fired with a satisfying racket. The Parade Committee got mislaid and as it was not clear where the parade was to start, it ended up with four or five separate parades, each vying with the others for the right of way. There was no baseball game that first Fourth of July in Skagway — the ball field was too far from the paint stores and the shell games were more fun and provided faster action, anyway. There was some argument over the outcome of the horse race, which was held on the beach at low tide. This made for a slow and muddy track and an old pack mule led the field. There were some who contended that a mule could not win a horse race, but the Stroller does not recall how it was settled, if it ever was. The big dance that night was held in a warehouse on the dock and there were three inspectors at the door — one to check on marriage licenses, one to gauge the sobriety of the applicants for admission,

53

and a third to bounce those rejected by the other two. The first two used discretion, while the latter used a sandbag.

The Finance Committee, upon which the success of the entire affair depended to a large extent, was very diligent and the local business houses were generous in their contributions, and by early in the afternoon of the Fourth the committee had on hand a total of $1250. And, since this was calculated to be slightly in excess of what would be required to pay the bills the following day, the trio making up the committee decided they were entitled to just one quart of champagne as a token of appreciation for their arduous labors. Certainly one quart of champagne for three men was not excessive and nobody could object.

The investment was made and the quart was encompassed. But champagne is a seductive drink, and it had the effect of causing the members of the Finance Committee to feel like new men. And, being hospitable fellows, they invested in a second quart with which to treat the new men they felt themselves to be. The second quart was so much of an improvement over the first that they had a third, and after that they lost count and began buying for everybody who happened along. They had started early in the afternoon and by the time the sun sank behind the mountains there was only $50 left of the original $1,250. After some serious if not sober discussion, they decided to recoup this deficit with a single throw at a roulette table, and the $50 was raked in by the courteous dealer.

No Fourth of July bills were settled the following day or on any other day, and they have not been settled in the twenty-eight years that have since elapsed. The Stroller has several times sent a statement, addressed to the Fourth of July Celebration at Skagway, but only once did he get a reply and then it was a note asking him how he got that way. And in truth, the Stroller has always been bothered more by the $5 he advanced out of his own pocket than by the $79.50 worth of printing, and he has always felt that he should not have put up the other half. But Soapy unfortunately got into a little trouble just four days after the celebration and died of it before the Stroller got around to presenting him with a claim.

And the Stroller has also been exceedingly grieved whenever he remembers that he was so busy supervising the greased pole exercises while the Finance Committee was playing host to all comers that he did not even get a swallow of champagne.

WHITE PASS CITY

FEW PEOPLE WHO ride the White Pass Railroad from Skagway, Alaska, to Whitehorse, Yukon Territory, in these days of peace and quiet are aware that at a point about four miles south of the Summit there flourished for six months during the year 1898 what was probably the toughest, rawest, most Godless town ever known in the North or anywhere else. It was called White Pass City and its name was the only decent thing about it. Its residents were mostly those who were considered, even then, too tough to live in Skagway, and anyone who knew Skagway in those days will understand what the residents of White Pass City must have been.

It was in August of 1898 that the late E. C. Hawkins, chief construction engineer for the White Pass Railroad, insisted that the Stroller journey to White Pass City to witness the blowing off of the face of the mountain just above it and where a right-of-way was being carved out of the solid rock. It was an impressive feat of engineering and the charge that was to remove the mountain's face consisted of four or five tons of dynamite. The blast was scheduled to take place sometime between noon of Saturday and noon of Sunday, and when the event was pulled off it was fully up to expectations in the way of noise and flying rock.

But it is not of dynamite explosions or rights-of-way that the Stroller is now writing, but rather of White Pass City as he found it and associated with it that Saturday afternoon and night. White Pass City consisted mostly of tents but it also had sixteen buildings constructed of lumber and muslin, principally muslin. There were seventeen saloons — one for each building and one at large. Many of the saloon proprietors were women, among them being Kate the Greaser, Nigger Liz, Three Star Molly and Gum Boot Kitty, and corralled together as they were on a scant two acres of ground, they gave the place considerable flavor and atmosphere.

The seventeenth saloon was located in a tent hotel which was called the International House, and actually there were two saloons although both were under the same management. It was a very long tent and the hotel was in the middle and there was a bar at each end so that you could not enter or leave the hotel section without "Coming Through the Rye." It was the most pretentious hotel in the place, and as the Stroller was to remain in White Pass City overnight, he engaged a bunk there. It was probably called the International because no color line was drawn, anybody being welcome that had the price, regardless of color, race or previous condition, which was mostly not mentioned. Bunks were a dollar a night in advance, with no extra charge for any livestock you might bring in with you — or for any that you might pack away, either.

The proprietor of the International House was Ham Grease Jimmy who had been widely known in Skagway where he boosted for some of the blackjack games and called the dances at the Mascotte Saloon until a lucky turn of a card enabled him to buy the tent and a few bottles of booze with which to start in business for himself.

It was at one of Ham Grease Jimmy's bars in the International House the first evening of his sojourn in the new town that the Stroller witnessed a gambling game he had never before seen. Neither has he seen it since. The participants were a number of packers, hundreds of whom

57

made the busy little town their headquarters. White Pass City was then at the end of the wagon road and many tons of goods were packed from there to the Summit, a distance of four miles, by horse, mule or burro trains.

About 6 o'clock that Saturday evening a party of five packers returned from a trip to the Summit and entered the International, walking straight to the bar (the Stroller has often observed that men walk straighter to than from bars). A discussion immediately arose as to whose turn it was to buy, and a novel system of gambling was suggested as the best and quickest way to settle the matter. From under the coat collar of one of the number — any of the five could have supplied what was necessary — a big "creeper" was carefully removed and placed on the bar. Each of the five men then turned his back to the bar and placed his elbows upon it. Ham Grease Jimmy stood behind the bar as referee and the one to whom the louse crawled was stuck for the drinks.

Later the same evening the Stroller acted as referee for a bare-knuckle fight between the Skylight Kid and Jawbone Harry, the question at issue being which of the two would share a bed that night with the Black Prince. The latter was a colored pugilist who had arrived earlier in the day from Skagway and secured a double bed at the International, half of which he had generously offered to the winner of the contest. After six rounds of hard and bloody fighting, the Stroller called it a draw and claimed the sleeping privileges for himself. And, as the Stroller already had a bunk, he was able to dispose of these privileges later in the evening for a dollar and six-bits, bunks being scarce in White Pass City that night.

The completion of the railroad to the Summit later that year removed the only excuse White Pass City had for occupying a place on the topography, and after its brief but turbulent career the last vestige of the town disappeared and pristine quiet was as completely restored as though it had never been disturbed.

Only a few weeks ago the Stroller was a passenger over the White Pass Railroad, which skirts the site of the once busy town. As he gazed from the coach window at the few remnants of civilization still visible — old and rust-caked stoves, a rag fluttering from a tent pole, and twelve or fifteen carloads of empty whiskey bottles — a feeling of sadness wiggled athwart his system and an unbidden tear ground-sluiced for itself a right-of-way down his wizened cheek. It was not because the wicked and boisterous little town was no more, as it could readily be spared, but because the Stroller suddenly realized that a quarter of a century had been rolled together and laid away on the shelf of Eternity since he had been invited to "name yours" by the unfortunate and losing member of that unholy quintette that had stood with their backs to and elbows on Ham Grease Jimmy's bar.

SKAGWAY NEWSPAPER DAYS

THE STROLLER recalls the days, as well as the nights, he spent in the raw but thriving town of Skagway, during which time he was employed first as a reporter and then as the assistant editor of a newspaper, chiefly as being extremely busy. There was always something going on in Skagway in that year of 1898, and a part of what went on was fit to print. Steamer after steamer pulled in at the docks and disgorged hundreds and thousands of gold-seekers bound for the Klondike. Most of them milled around town for several days before starting over the pass and it was so common for them to be relieved of their money, either in the brightly lighted gambling houses or in the dimly lighted alleys of Skagway, that such an event was not considered news at all.

Law and order were very little known in Skagway at that time, and that little was known unfavorably. It was a time of vigilante committees, and committees to counter the work of the vigilantes. That was the year a snowslide on the Chilkoot Trail killed more than forty people but did not create nearly so much interest as the killing of one man in Skagway a few months later, the one man being Jefferson Randolph Soapy Smith. And there were many other important and historic events in Skagway that year, including the hair-yanking match between Cross-eyed Liz and Gin Sling Molly one evening at the Palace of Delight, the start of construction of the White Pass Railroad, and the elopement of the lady bartender at the Red Onion Saloon with one of the town's prominent merchants. In fact, as the Stroller remembers it, there was always more news in Skagway at that time than there was room for in her newspapers.

The newspaper office in which the Stroller was employed was sandwiched between two important emporiums of trade on Fifth Avenue. The place on one side carried a sign with the single word PAINT, and although there was not a can of paint on its shelves, there was a plentiful supply of the kind of "thinner" used in painting the town red. The place on the other side advertised GENTS' FURNISHINGS but carried exactly the same kind of goods as the paint store. In the same block there were two saloons, with blackjack and faro tables on the side, and a dancehall. It was a busy block; sometimes too busy.

There was the night a man was killed in the Klondike Saloon and the stranger who did the shooting fled to the street, pursued by a crowd of enraged friends of the deceased. Five shots were fired at him just as he passed the printing office, but none of them made connections with their target. Two struck the sidewalk and three penetrated the newspaper building in which the Stroller was asleep. And while none of the bullets found their way to his pallet under the press, the next morning the Stroller took the precaution of securing several sheets of boiler iron with which to surround his boudoir.

Thus it was with some misgivings that the Stroller accepted, a couple of months later, the promotion to assistant editor of the paper, for in that elevated position he would do his slumbering on a cot in a corner of the editorial office. But as no bullets had recently entered the office and the cot was more comfortable than the lowly pallet, he made the move. A few mornings later he was awakened by violent hammering on the wall close to his ear, and when he turned over he could see a huge spike coming through the partition. It kept coming until a full eight inches protruded over the pillow, whereupon the Stroller hastily dressed and went next door to the paint store to learn the whys and wherefors. It turned out that no harm had been intended. The spike was being used to anchor a sardine can to the wall for use as a soap dish, and at the Stroller's request it was withdrawn and a carpet tack substituted.

Like most newspapers the world around, the paper to which the Stroller devoted his hours of toil maintained a Society Column, but the producing of it was an uphill job in Skagway. Few families had yet settled there, and since the portion of society that slept under the gaming tables was rigidly excluded from the society news, there was little to draw on. Even marriages, the old stand-by of the society news reporter, had to be handled carefully. Old-fashioned people take the matter of marrying and giving in marriage seriously and are anxious for full and detailed write-ups to appear in their local newspaper. But not many old-fashioned people then resided in Skagway. It was a free, unfettered and impulsive populace, and marriage was merely an incident, as like to happen as not to, depending on the recognition accorded the conventionalities by the people concerned. It was not unusual for an avowed and sworn celibate to arise in the morning firm and steadfast in his principles, and before repose again overtook him anything might have happened, including marriage. And in such event, he was more than likely not to want news of it to appear in print.

Even when there were no such impediments, news of a wedding was not always easy to report in full detail. The Stroller, for example, was called into a saloon one morning, invited to name his pizen, and informed by the hospitable bartender that he had been married the night before.

"What was the name of your bride?" inquired the Stroller, hauling out his notebook.

The new bridegroom scratched his head. He looked up and thought for a minute, then he looked down and thought for another minute. Finally he polished the bar and thought some more.

"Here," he said at last. "You tend bar and I'll run over and ask her. I heard it, but I forget what it was. You'll find rye and Scotch on ice under the bar."

All in all, the Stroller had few dull moments during those months, for in addition to his ordinary newspaper duties he was expected to assist with various causes and civic enterprises sponsored or promoted by the newspaper. One of these causes was the organization and financing of the Skagway Fire Department, for the town had no fire department and no regular fire-fighting equipment. Tents and shacks had been catching fire and burning to cinders from the day the town first burst into bud, but when saloons and dancehalls also began to go up in smoke there was a hue and cry for a fire department, as such losses were held to be bad for business. Under ordinary circumstances a fire department would have been the concern and responsibility of the municipal government, but there were few ordinary circumstances in Skagway and there was no municipal government. There was, in fact, no law in Alaska at that time under which a municipal corporation could be organized.

So the fire department had to be a voluntary civic affair and the newspaper on which the Stroller labored spearheaded the movement, with the Stroller on the point of the spear a good part of the time. The organization of the department itself presented few problems. Volunteer firemen were numerous and they quickly elected a fire chief and a couple of captains, while contributions from the business houses took care of the purchase of half a gross of red flannel shirts, two or three ladders, a dozen fire buckets and some axes – especially axes.

But what was really needed was a pumping engine and some hose, and to raise the money for this it was decided to hold a benefit entertainment. A committee was formed and a manager, a treasurer and a publicity agent were appointed. The latter position fell to the Stroller and he was happy to accept as he knew he would have to write promotional stories for his paper, anyway. But the Stroller did not foresee that the treasurer would be stricken with pneumonia or that the manager would leave town suddenly and under circumstances never fully explained. This left the entire burden upon the Stroller's quivering shoulders.

It had been agreed that the show should have professional direction and a man and his wife were employed to drill the cast and instruct the members in stage demeanor, voice modulation and when to appear and disappear. The couple had come north with the blissful anticipation of pulling down $300 a week in a vaudeville show, but their first appearance had raised such insistent and continuous demands from the audience for the hook that they resigned and consented to direct the fire department benefit. It was a meal ticket, if only a temporary one, and a meal ticket was what that couple stood most in need of at the time.

A number of other professional entertainers were out of work just then and the directors suggested that it would be a good idea to hire some of them to do specialty numbers in the show, as they would work for nominal pay just to tide themselves over until something better showed up. The result was that by the time the entertainment was ready for presentation there were something like forty people in the cast, although the main feature of the evening, a tear-starting drama entitled "The Blacksmith" only called for eight. One reason "The Blacksmith" was selected was that the leading man, provided with half a dozen anvils and a couple of hammers, could pound out "Rock of Ages" or some other patriotic number any time a member of the cast forgot his lines and thus cover the lapse.

The show was generously supported, some 1,250 tickets being sold at $1 each for the 500 seats in the house, and it was well received by the audience. the leading man was kept busy on the anvils until his arm nearly dropped off, the male quartet was called back for two encores, and the specialty numbers, particularly those by the Ping Pong Kid, Little Tuskawilla, and a girl from Wyoming who called herself the Queen of the Skimmed Milk Ranch, were riots.

As the expenses of the production, including the salaries of the directors, were under $300, the affair was also declared a glowing financial success and the chief of the fire department was so carried away by it that he suggested to the Stroller, after the performance, that the entire cast be taken to the Pack Train Restaurant for a midnight supper. The Stroller remembers many fool suggestions that have been made to him as he struggled down life's rugged pathway, but he fails to recall one that was more foolish.

Tony and Louie, the proprietors of the Pack Train, had but one hour to prepare the repast, and the Stroller has been thankful ever since that they did not have two hours. The Stroller squirmed when everybody ordered fried chicken, and he writhed when they began ordering Mumm's, which was then $10 per quart in Skagway. The capacity of that cast was phenomenal and if the Stroller squirmed at fried chicken and writhed at champagne, he passed into spasms when orders for the latter were repeated with utter abandon. The Stroller had seen thirsts before and he has seen thirsts since, but never has he seen thirsts as difficult to assuage as those assembled at the Pack Train on that memorable night.

After the champagne had been flowing freely for a time the atmosphere in the Pack Train became most exhilarating and some of the guests began to display talents the Stroller had not known they possessed and which they may not themselves have suspected. Little Egypt did a hoochy-coochy on a table and she — well, the Stroller cannot claim to be a connoisseur of the hoochy-coochy, but he has never seen one like it, and he noticed that the eyes of both Tony and Louie were close to popping from their heads. The Skim Milk Queen did cartwheels down the length of the counter but she overestimated its length and a wheelbarrow was required to carry her to her boudoir in the attic over a butcher shop.

When the supper started at midnight, the Stroller could see the fire department's benefit fund begin to ooze away, and as the night progressed he noticed that it was no longer oozing but was gushing and gurgling merrily. By 4 o'clock he had lost all hope that there would be anything for the fire department, and by 5 o'clock he was wondering how much the fire department would be in the hole. But there was no cause for worry. After Tony had added up the bill and it had been settled there was a balance of $13.75 left of the original $1,250.

This balance was turned over to the fire department at its regular meeting two nights later and was received with a rousing vote of thanks to all who had participated in the benefit show. All agreed that it had been a scintillating affair, but the Stroller was a nervous wreck and wished that he had never heard of "The Blacksmith" or the Skagway Fire Department either.

Only a few days later the Stroller picked up a copy of one of the Dawson newspapers and observed that it not only did not support and applaud its local fire department, but actually opposed, derided and roasted it at every opportunity. And the Stroller decided, then and there, that Dawson was the place for him.

A TRIP
ON A SCOW

WHEN THE STROLLER decided late in the fall of 1898 to move his headquarters from Skagway to Dawson, a distance of nearly six hundred miles, it was necessary for him to find the most economical means of transportation for himself, his wife and their small daughter. The reason for this was that while the Stroller had, during his months in Skagway, come to be looked upon as a substantial and upright citizen, his financial substance was barely visible to the naked eye and his uprightness had failed to provide the price of two full fares and a half fare to Dawson by steamboat.

Four different modes of transportation came into use before the long trip ended. The first part, from Skagway to the Summit, was made on the White Pass Railroad which was being pushed as rapidly as possible to Bennett and then on to Whitehorse. The next stretch, from the Summit to Bennett, which was for all practical purposes the extreme head of navigation on the Yukon, was made in a jolting freight wagon and the best part of it was that the distance was not far. And at Bennett the Stroller shipped on a scow, which was bound for Dawson with a load of freight, as an able seaman and with the privilege of taking his family with him. Of course, the Stroller was not an able seaman or even an ordinary seaman, but it turned out that neither was anybody else on board, although they all claimed to be, and his deception was never mentioned.

Two scows left Bennett together for the trip across the lakes and down the river to Dawson and they managed to keep fairly close together during the voyage. There were ten men on each scow and the Stroller's wife and daughter made a total of twelve people on the one, which was laden with mining machinery, a piano and general merchandise. The other one carried mining machinery and forty live hogs. At least, they were live at the start, as their squeals gave ample notice to anyone within earshot. But hog cholera broke out among them and half of them died along the way. The others were more dead than alive but could still emit squeals when they reached Dawson, where they were promptly sold and butchered before they keeled over and turned up their toenails. The Stroller did not eat pork that winter in Dawson; he had lost his appetite for it, and anyway he could not afford the asking price.

The scow on which the Stroller was employed was a big open box with a narrow deck along each side and a short deck at each end. There were two big sweeps on each side to help move the scow along and an even bigger sweep at each end to steer it with. At least that was the theory of the end sweeps, but like a great many theories, the practical application wasn't anything to brag about. The steering went fine until the scow took a notion to turn around and this happened, on the average, about every ten minutes. Once the scow started a turn it could not be stopped by the application of all six sweeps, and the crew soon gave up trying and let it swing a hundred and eighty degrees and tried to catch it there. In consequence, while the scow went pretty steadily down the river, it was a kind of revolving progress with sometimes one end first and sometimes the other, and much of the time it was broadside. There was also a mast, a big square of canvas for a sail, and a crossarm which the knowing ones called a yard and which could be hoisted to the top of the mast to spread the sail. These were for use on broad reaches of the river when there was a favoring wind and in crossing the numerous lakes.

The Stroller will not say that the scow hit every rock in the Yukon between Bennett and Dawson because he does not know how many rocks there are in that stretch of the river. It did hit a great many rocks and he sometimes wondered, when the scow went into its turning act, whether it was trying to go back and make a swipe at a rock it had missed. When it hit a rock there was a heart-stopping crash, then a bumping and thumping while it slid on over. No serious damage resulted but the Stroller cannot say that he ever got used to it or enjoyed it. Sandbars were almost as numerous as rocks and while they were not as scary and nerve-jolting, there was usually more work connected with hitting one of them. Grounding on a sandbar was accompanied by a gentle, sliding crunch and then the scow came to a dead stop. Poles were used to shove off when possible but often it was necessary for part or all of the crew to wade into the river and shove. This was late in the fall and that Yukon River water was invigorating; a two minute waist-deep application of it would keep a man shivering for a couple of hours.

There are some wicked rapids on the upper Yukon but when the scow reached them a pair of professional river pilots came aboard to see us through and in their hands the scow settled down and became as docile as an old cow and the rapids were passed without incident. But a few days later the help of a pilot or even just an experienced seaman would have been a great comfort in crossing one of the lakes. The day started quietly enough with a light and favoring breeze. The sail was hoisted and the scow began to move slowly but steadily across the lake. Soon the wind increased and the scow moved faster and everybody was pleased, for a time. But the wind continued to strengthen and it rolled up waves which grew higher and higher and came charging down the lake in endless white-capped ranks. The scow pitched and rolled and wallowed and

69

water began to come over the sides and both ends. There were ten men aboard and nine different opinions about what should be done. The tenth man, who had been designated the captain, didn't have an opinion but kept wringing his hands and lamenting that his poor wife would never know what had become of him.

Finally it was suggested that the sail be lowered but this was taken care of by the wind which snapped off the mast and blew the canvas away completely. The scow then turned broadside to the waves and wallowed worse than ever. At times it threatened to roll over, but the utmost effort with the sweeps failed to turn the scow from its broadside position. Then a steamer came along and her captain, with a great jangling of bells and snorting of her engines, brought her close to the scow. He yelled for everyone to jump and to hurry up about it because he couldn't risk staying there for long. Nobody jumped. The Stroller wanted his wife to go but she didn't like the looks of the four or five feet of churning gray water between the scow and the steamer and while they argued one of the men picked up the little girl and tossed her to waiting arms on the deck of the steamer. Then the captain was heard to say something about "utter fools" and he backed his vessel away and was gone.

After a time the wind and waves went down and eventually the scow reached the lower end of the lake. The steamer had gone on but the little girl had been left with some people who were camped on the shore there. She was glad to see her parents, but she had a pressing question to ask them.

"What is an orphan?" she wanted to know.

"Why do you want to know that?" said her mother.

"Because, those nice people on the boat seemed very sad and they kept looking back and saying, 'Surely she must be an orphan by this time.'"

All this time the scow was moving northward and it was

getting later and later in the year. One morning there was a skim of ice around the scow and the following morning it was more than a skim. The ice soon built up around the scow in a solid cake and it became impossible to use the sweeps and there was nothing to do but drift along with the ice. It was helpful in one way because the scow never hung up on the sandbars but slid over them on the ice, with an extra push from the ice building up behind. The ice got thicker and before long it filled the river from bank to bank. It kept moving, grinding along the banks and breaking up into cakes when the river narrowed or made a sharp bend, but the cakes quickly froze together again. The scow was locked in the ice for the last hundred miles or so and progress grew slower and slower and finally stopped altogether some fifteen miles above Dawson. There was nothing to do then but to try to keep warm and wait for the ice to thicken enough for travel. The Stroller salvaged some odds and ends of lumber from around the scow and built a sled. Since he was approximately as handy with tools as a young black bear, it was quite a sled — strong but not much for looks. Nevertheless, it served the purpose and he loaded his wife and their child on it with their belongings and trudged into Dawson on the end of a rope. that was the fourth mode of transportation and from the Stroller's viewpoint it was the least satisfactory of them all, but the little girl enjoyed it and shouted encouragement all the way.

Even now when he raises his hands from his No. 10 Remington typewriter and examines the remains of the callouses left by those sweeps, the Stroller is glad he made that trip. It gave him something to brag about to people who made the entire journey to Dawson by comfortable river steamer and whose greatest hardship was that they sometimes slept through the dinner gong and missed a meal. But he would not make the trip on a scow again for the whole Klondike with a fence around it.

PARTNERS

THE ENORMOUS LABORS required in moving an outfit over the trail and then down the Yukon to the Klondike during the days of the big Gold Rush were highly conducive to the formation of partnerships, as in many instances one man alone was all but helpless. Two men were essential, for example, in working the heavy whip-saws with which lumber was cut for the building of boats at the head of navigation. A boat could be put together by two men in much less than half the time required by one man alone. And the boat, if it was capable of floating at all when finished, would carry two outfits as readily as one.

But the trials and tribulations of the trail and the river were such that partnerships were sundered almost as readily as they were formed. Probably there is no hatred on earth more bitter and more corrosive than that which was bred by the familiarity and the enforced association of two partners travelling the Klondike Trail. Men who had been friends for years and whose individual interests were completely interlocked, at least until they could reach Dawson, would quarrel savagely and split up along the way. The boat would be sawed apart, leaving two useless halves. Tents were split down the middle, stoves were torn apart, and even candles were meticulously cut exactly in half in tragic and childish partings that happened hundreds of times along that rugged route.

Unfortunately, this kind of behaviour did not limit itself to the trail but frequently extended to the gold fields as well when two men essayed to work a claim in partnership, and especially if the claim was in an isolated location.

The Stroller remembers two men whom he will call Tom and Jack. They had reached the Klondike together from Skagway without undue friction and had staked a rich claim on a distant creek. And there they worked together amiably as they built a cabin, moved in their outfit and started sinking their first hole to bedrock.

Then the winter of '99 shut down, isolating them from other miners, and before long they had quarreled. The Stroller does not know what started the quarrel. It was probably something trivial, but that did not make it any the less bitter. Before long they had divided the cabin by drawing a line down the middle and whacked up the grub supply into two equal parts, one of which was placed in each end of the cabin. At enormous labor they sledded in a second stove so that each could cook what he wanted and when he wanted it. They used the single door in common but otherwise they lived as completely separate lives as though they had been separated by a mile instead of by an invisible partition. Each completely ignored the other when they were in the cabin.

This was not possible when they were at work, but they did continue to work the claim, which yielded a good deal of gold and which was also divided evenly. And, since the work did require some communication between them, they invented a mythical third partner to help out with it. They called him Joe.

"Joe, will you tell Jack to crank up the windlass. The bucket's full," Tom would say. Or Jack would say, "Joe, you tell Tom not to load that bucket so heavy. I ain't no mule."

And so the long and dreary winter dragged on. Then the gay and glorious days of spring arrived and one sunny morning Jack finished breakfast, put on his hat and, addressing Tom directly for the first time in months, said: "I'm going to town." But Tom neither looked up nor acknowledged that he had heard.

Two hours after Jack reached town he was watching the play at the faro layout in the Monte Carlo, listening joyously to the sounds of voices around him and freely rubbing elbows with his fellow men. Then Tom also entered the Monte Carlo, walked directly to Jack, and said: "Have you anything valuable or that you care about in your end of the cabin?"

It took Jack by surprise for a moment but he quickly recovered and asked: "What in hell business is it of yours whether or not I have anything valuable in my end of the cabin?"

"You are perfectly right," said Tom, turning on his heel. "It is none of my business what you have in your end of the cabin. But I thought it only fair to tell you that I set fire to my end of the cabin before I left."

But not every shipwrecked partnership remained permanently on the rocks, and the Stroller recalls at least one that was patched and cemented together again, apparently as good as new.

It was in January of 1900 that Ham Grease Jimmy and the No Shirt Kid, both previously well known around Skagway, arrived in Dawson. They had made the long trip over the lakes and rivers from Bennett, a distance approaching five hundred miles, and had necked a handsled containing their worldly chattels all that distance. Despite the fact that they had quarrelled constantly during their six weeks' journey, they could not divide up and separate. All their flour was in one sack and they had but one fur robe under which to sleep. The result was that when they reached Dawson they hated each other with a murderous hatred. But they had heard of and had wholesome respect for British justice as meted out by the Royal Northwest Mounted Police, and neither of them was anxious to take a chance of having to work for six months or a year on the Crown Fuel Reduction Plant, as the big woodpile behind the police barracks was sometimes known.

Both men were worn to a frazzle when they reached Dawson and they devoted their first week in the Yukon metropolis to eating and sleeping, each with the sole object of gaining strength enough to give the other a lambasting that would be remembered to the grave. What followed is best told just as Ham Grease Jimmy gave it to the Stroller:

"Dis mornin' I wakes up an' I sees No Shirt lookin' at me wid murder in his peepers, an' I says to him, "We might as well settle dis t'ing today as any time.' So we agrees to take de sled an' go down de river aways an' fight it out, de victor to haul de vanquished back to town on de sled.

"About 10 o'clock we starts out, an' when we gets opposite de high bluff below town de light is just gettin' right for fightin'. No time is lost, see? At it we goes.

"'Take dat,' I says, 'for de time you harpooned four of de six slices of bacon out of de skillet, den spit in de skillet when you t'ot I wasn't lookin', an' I closes his right lamp.

"'An' take dat,' I says, 'for pretendin' to be sick so I hauls you on de sled all de way from Hellsgate to Selkirk,' and I dislocates his left ear.

"'An take dat,' I says, 'for de night below Pelly when you stole all de robe but about a foot an' near froze me to death,' an I puts his other lamp on de bum.

"An' den I puts all me remainin' strength into a straight punch an' caves in his nose, an' I says, 'An' dat is for all your general cussedness from de day we left Bennett 'til we hits Dawson.'

"But don't you t'ink for a minute dat No Shirt ain't got fight in him. Man, dat bird can fight like a wildcat, an' as evidence of dat statement, just give me de once-over. He

75

ain't no skirt, lemme tell you. He's all I want to tackle, an' I have more respect for him now dan I ever had before. From now on, me an' him is partners an' he can have anyt'ing I got."

And Ham Grease Jimmy kept his word. He had hauled the temporarily blinded No Shirt Kid back to town on the handsled and told the police his friend had slipped off the bluff below town and battered himself up in the fall. Then he called a doctor to brace up No Shirt's nose, pin his ear back on, and otherwise repair his features. And while time and arnica were doing their work, Ham Grease Jimmy continued to eat bacon and at the same time paid two dollars a pound for beefsteak with which to poultice No Shirt's eyes.

It was three weeks later that Ham Grease Jimmy and the No Shirt Kid called at the Stroller's office to bid him good-bye.

"So long, old Scribblin' Pal," they chorused. "We is off to Nome wid our outfit on de same old sled, an' on dis trip dere won't be no sidesteppin' from duty. Everyt'ing is goin' to be fifty-fifty."

"An' dere won't be no spittin' in de skillet, neider, see?" added Ham Grease Jimmy.

FIRE
IN
DAWSON

WHAT WOULD THE early-day reporters of Dawson, the Stroller included, have used for news stories had it not been for the fires that continually plagued that thriving Klondike gold camp? The Stroller cannot answer this question because he never encountered the problem. There were plenty of fires in Dawson. Three times within a year and a half large sections of the town were swept away by flames, and it was an off morning that did not produce at least one fire. And the fact that the worst fire season was in the winter when other news was often scarce was beneficial to the reporters and the newspapers, if to nobody else.

One of the things that contributed to the large number of winter fires was the fact that the town supported a number of professional fire-builders. They were not arsonists, although in many instances their work had much the same result. These fellows made a living by engaging to build fires for those who could afford their services and were averse to crawling out of a warm bed on sub-zero mornings to start their own fires. The fire-builder made his rounds in the early morning hours and at each dwelling on his route he kindled the fire, opened the draft and the damper to make sure it blazed merrily, and then went on to the next place to repeat the chore. And often he performed his duties so well that, there being no one awake to turn down the damper when the stove grew hot, the floor, wall or ceiling caught fire and the occupants of the place were forced to flee into the bitter cold in what they had on, which was sometimes very little.

While fires constituted an important part of the news during the quiet months of a Dawson winter, the amount of space devoted to any particular fire was governed, at least in part, by the quantity of other news that happened to be available. Thus, on a day when it had to compete with the suicide of a dancehall girl or a sensational shooting, a sizeable fire might receive little space in the papers. On the other hand, when little else was going on, a small and insignificant fire in a cabin might receive a full headline and several columns of type.

The Stroller particularly recalls one fire that the Dawson news reporters wrote up at far greater length and with more detail than it deserved on its own merits as news, while the stories themselves brought on events that were never contemplated by their writers. This fire started at about 7:30 o'clock one winter morning in a cabin only a block from what was known as "newspaper row" from the fact that more than a dozen men connected with the town's three daily papers lived there. As a result of this proximity, nearly every reporter in town was on hand.

The occupants of the cabin, a man and a woman, were somewhat singed before they could escape, although neither was seriously injured. The man operated a wheel at Nigger Jim's New Pavilion and the woman was a dancer in the same establishment. It made a good story but not an important one, and ordinarily it would not have rated more than four inches of space on the second page. But on that day the telegraph line was out of commission, there had been no mail for three weeks, and news of any kind was scarce. So the reporters, each of whom was required to fill a certain number of columns every day whether or not there was any real news to fill them with, turned themselves loose and gave the fire story their full attention.

There were thrilling descriptions of the blazing holocaust, the work of the gallant firemen, the heroic rescue efforts and finally of the couple's dash to safety with the tails of their "retiring apparel" curtailed by the cruel flames. All possible details were dredged up and woven into the stories. Included were the names of the principals and of the man who first discovered the fire, the people who spread the alarm, the firemen, the women who furnished coffee to the firemen, and some of the bystanders who actually had nothing to do with it but whose names helped to fill space. The story was on the front page of all the papers, under the largest headlines available. These headlines were always something of a problem for the paper which employed the Stroller because of a shortage of the letter "K" in its font of 72-point type, and the Stroller has looked upon the headline he wrote that day as a masterpiece. It filled the space, it told the story, and it did not use a single letter K:

ROULETTE DEALER
IS GIVEN WHIFF
OF HEREAFTER

Now, there are people everywhere who cannot mind their own business, and Dawson was no exception. One of the many people who read the fire story that day was a woman who had known the singed operator on the Outside and had also known his wife and children. She bought several copies of that day's edition of each of the papers and mailed them, one at a time and spaced out over a period of several weeks, to the wife, figuring that if one paper got lost enroute another would surely arrive. She paid twenty-five cents each for the papers and what she paid in postage charges the Stroller does not know, but it must have been considerable.

At least one of the papers did reach the wife, and when navigation opened on the upper Yukon about the 10th of the following June, she was on the Whitehorse dock with her suitcase in her hand. She reached Dawson on the first steamer of the year to furrow the melting ice of Lake Lebarge, and at Dawson she stopped, looked and listened. Then she hurried back to Seattle and called a divorce lawyer the moment her steamer docked.

And that was not the only Dawson fire that had consequences that were entirely unforeseen at the time. As a result of one fire, the Stroller enjoyed the greatest triumph of his newspaper career. He was challenged to a duel. And he followed this triumph with another when he drew upon the great store of wit and ingenuity he constantly keeps on tap, to escape the challenge without the loss of a drop of either blood or honor. But before he releases these thrilling details to a waiting world, the Stroller should explain what it was that attracted him to the Klondike gold capital in the first place.

Dawson in those halcyon years had many attractions for many different kinds of people, not the least of these attractions being the gold fields at her back door. But the thing that drew the Stroller's attention to Dawson and influenced him to move there was the discovery that one of its newspapers roasted the local fire department, habitually and as a matter of policy, at every opportunity, for in Skagway he had grown weary of writing stories that praised the fire department even when it merited the exact opposite. At Dawson the Stroller secured employment on this attractive paper and the first instructions he received were that he was to pan the fire department and give it what-for every time he got the chance, and to see to it that the chances were frequent. Those were standing orders and the Stroller heeded them to the best of his ability, with the natural result that his popularity with the members of the department was very scanty.

Another newsman, a fellow named George, arrived in Dawson about the same time as the Stroller and went to work for a rival paper, one that had a policy of devoting a good deal of space to boosting the fire department. Early one morning a few weeks later a fire broke out in a shell of a building occupied by a hardware store and both the Stroller and George were on the scene. In the darkness and smoke and confusion, some of the firemen mistook George for "that smart aleck Yankee that is always panning us." They gave the fire a rest and turned the hose on George, and as the mercury was away down in the basement he soon resembled the centerpiece at an ice carnival.

This of course presented the Stroller with another opportunity and in that evening's paper he "gave it" to the fire department for careless handling of the hose, inattention to duty, wasting precious water, poor sportsmanship and failure to save the store building. He also advised the victim to bring suit, and this was done. But the only money that changed hands was the $100 George paid a lawyer, as the jury decided it was not George's fire and he had no business there. George at once quit his job on the paper and went to boosting for a blackjack game. He said he would rather boost there than boost a fire department that would turn the hose on him.

Later that same winter one of the firemen, a fellow who couldn't keep a good thing to himself, put George wise to what had happened. It was all a mistake, the fireman told him, and it was the Stroller they had really intended to drown. It was then that George challenged the Stroller to a duel. Dueling was illegal to the Yukon and the Royal Northwest Mounted Police were very diligent about stopping such affairs when they came to their attention, so all the arrangements would have to be made secretly. The Stroller, as the challenged party, had the choice of weapons and after giving the matter some study he picked fire hoses, with the man who could stand up under the heaviest load of ice to be declared the winner. Poor George, his teeth rattling at the very thought of another turn under the hose, backed down. The Stroller had been sure George would back down, but as a precaution he had also tipped off the police.

POLICE
COURT

THE NEWSPAPER MAN views all the events and happenings of life from one particular point of view, and that is their worth as interesting stories. The world at large may deplore a certain happening in which a newspaper man will rejoice, his joy arising from the fact that the happening possesses all the essentials of a good and interesting and sometimes sensational news story.

No doubt the world at large rejoiced to read, in a Dawson paper of recent date, that only one case was tried before the Police Court of that city during the month of January, a month which contained thirty-one days. But in the Stroller that simple news item produced a sadness which, while it may be mellowed by time, will never be entirely effaced. For in the early and lively days of Dawson, her Police Court was her most prolific source of news and hence it was very dear to the hearts of the news reporters who toiled there.

The Stroller might say that in those glorious years it was relatively easy to get into jail in Dawson and hence to occupy a place on the Anxious Seat in her Police Court. It was the custom to put a man in jail, then investigate to see if there was anything on which to hold him. If nothing could be found, he was dismissed with a warning to watch his step and told that he was lucky to have such a good reputation but not to do it again.

It was, in fact, so easy to get into jail that an interesting and rare curio in the Dawson Museum is a photograph of eleven men who passed through the ordeal of pioneer days in the town without once being put behind the steel bars. The Stroller is in that picture, but the secret of how he was able to accomplish this he will reveal later. When the picture was taken an attempt was made to include twelve men in it, but eleven were all that were found who could qualify and the effort to make it a "Lucky Dozen" was unavailing. Of the eleven, four fell from grace in Dawson after the picture was taken, three were found to be living under assumed names, and two left the country with helpmeets who had been preempted by other men. This left only the Stroller and one other at whom the unmanicured finger of scorn could not be pointed, and even they had hard work maintaining the reputation they had advertised in the picture. In fact, keeping up his reputation began to tell on the Stroller's health and that was one of his prime reasons for eventually leaving Dawson.

But the Stroller started to tell of the Dawson Police Court, which he covered as a part of his beat for nearly five years. It was a busy and productive place in those years and it was an off day that it was not good for at least a column of spicy reading matter. By studying the habits of many who frequented the Lonesome Bench, the Stroller could invariably tell, even before he entered court in the morning, which of the regulars was due for a hearing. For this purpose he kept his own "jag book" in which the names of the "periodics" and the "intermittents" were entered. By consulting this book he could determine just who should be on the docket for that day. Now and then one of the regulars would become derelict, but when the Stroller called such a lapse to the attention of the delinquent, the latter almost always showed up the following morning with that dark brown taste protruding from the corners of his mouth.

The excuses offered in Police Court for having

encompassed an overdose of hootch, much of which was hand made and very powerful, were often original and sometimes unique. One man would swear that he had arrived in town from the creeks nearly frozen and had taken less than "two fingers" to thaw out on, only to wake up as a guest in the lockup. Another would assert that he had met a friend just back from the Outside and had celebrated the meeting with "just one for friendship's sake." And the Stroller once heard an Irishman offer the excuse that "Oi just came from the creeks and heard the Pope had died an' tuck a couple of wee dhrops to dhrown me sorrows, yer Worship."

"Cramps" were worked heavily as an excuse for overindulgence. "I was all doubled up and suffering great pain, your Lordship, and I took only a small touch for the good of my stomach" was heard on an average of twice a week. And if one made this plea convincing enough to obtain dismissal, the same spiel was tried by every incarcerated drunk during the week following.

Dual names created some difficulties on those days when Police Court news was heavy and every bit of it was published. For example, there were two men in Dawson by the name of Alex Ross. One was quiet and temperate and knew not the appearance of red whiskey when it reared up on its hind legs in a glass, while the other was a "periodic" who played two engagements each month before the judge. The name Alex Ross would appear regularly in the news columns and the temperate Alex would just as regularly publish a "card" the following day to explain that the Alex Ross fined for drunkenness was not the Alex Ross of untarnished name and reputation but another man entirely. This notice appeared so regularly, in fact, that the temperate Alex was given a special annual rate and the "card" was kept standing in type, ready for use at any time the other Alex saw fit to cultivate a red plush jag.

The Police Court in those years averaged ten cases a day every day in the week except Sunday and Monday. On Sunday there were none and on Monday there was a double-header. On Mondays the Stroller has seen as many as twenty on the "lonesome bench" at one time. In those days misery not only loved company but had plenty of it. In addition to the "periodics" and the "intermittents" there were hundreds of others who played one night stands in the Dawson lockup and after "treatment" before the judge next morning were never seen there again. They either reformed or moved to some other place where they could drink and be merry without being molested.

The question naturally arises: What has happened in Dawson to shrink its Police Court business from upward of three hundred cases in a month to a single case in the same period? The population today is smaller than it was when the Stroller was making notations in his "jag book," it is true, but it has not dwindled in anywhere near that proportion. The police may have lost their vigilance, but it seems doubtful. Nor does the Stroller opine that the intake of whiskey, on a per capita basis, is less than formerly, although the quality of the product being dispensed today may be higher than the hand made valley tan of early years.

But after due consideration of all the facts available to him, the Stroller cannot help but feel that he himself may be responsible for the heavy blow the news reporters of Dawson have suffered. The Stroller was present in the Dawson Police Court on several hundred occasions without ever coming under the necessity of making excuses to the judge and he attributes this entirely to the fact that he always and under all circumstances put a squirt of lemon in it. He also exhorted his fellow residents to do likewise, but during his years in Dawson these words went unheeded, and he left there feeling that his uplift work had been in vain. But it now appears that his endeavors have at long last borne fruit and that the squirt of lemon has all but put the Dawson Police Court on the superannuation list.

One single case during the long month of January! Unfortunately, the news item carried no details about this lonely case and the Stroller has no idea what it amounted to. But he does clearly recall the details of one case he listened to in that court on a crisp morning in the early Fall of 1900. The Anxious Seat had gradually emptied until only one man, a tall, rawboned miner, remained. When his name was called and he was asked whether he had anything to say for himself, he shuffled forward and entered this plea:

"Your Lordship, in the month of May I was out on my claim, busy shoveling into the sluice-box for my winter clean-up. And when the birthday of the good Queen came around, there was naught within many miles with which to make the customary toast to her good health and well being. Nor did I then have the time to go after the necessary, for as your Lordship is aware, the season when the waters flow and a clean-up can be made is very brief. But the omission weighed heavily upon me all during the following months and I made up my mind that I would repair the neglect at the first opportunity. That opportunity came last evening, your Lordship, when I arrived in town. As a result of my feelings about the matter, so long pent up, I may have overdone the honors, but it was all for the good health of the Queen, may the Saints preserve her."

"Case dismissed," said the judge, entirely unaware that the tall miner was a native of West Virginia and had never heard of Queen Victoria until he reached the Klondike.

GRIST
FOR THE
NEWSMILL

WHEN THE Stroller reached Dawson, in the heart of the Klondike gold fields, late in the year 1898, he found many of the same class of people he had previously known in Skagway. In fact, many of them were the same individuals, and their activities were producing much the same line-up of news the Stroller had become familiar with in Skagway. But there was this major difference between the two towns: Skagway was open to shipping the year around, so there was a continuous flow of news from the outside world with which to fill the columns of the newspapers. Dawson, on the other hand, was virtually isolated for long periods during the winter.

Mail came over the winter trail from Skagway once a month — when it could make it. The longest period between mails after regular service was established, as the Stroller remembers it, was thirty-three days — late in the year 1899. There was also the Dominion telegraph line which carried press dispatches, at the rate of eight cents a word, when the line was working. But it was out of commission much of the time. Most of the line ran through wilderness country and a tree might fall across the wire or a moose would tangle his horns in it forty or fifty miles from anywhere. Then the linemen would have to hike out to locate the break and repair it, and this required from a day to a week and sometimes longer.

One result of this lack of mail and telegraph service was that much of the news in the Dawson papers was necessarily home grown and hand picked. There were three daily papers in Dawson for some time, with a great deal of rivalry among them for the attention of the newspaper-buying public, their circulation depending heavily on individual sales both on the streets of the town and out along the maze of creeks where the miners worked. Sales were promoted by the use of large and sensational headlines in all the papers, and the front page of the paper on which the Stroller was employed regularly carried three headlines, of three lines each and in the largest type in the shop. Composing these headlines was something of a problem on this paper because of the scarcity of the letter "K" in the 72-point font, only three being available. This was a serious handicap as in those days there was at least one King of the Klondike on every street corner in Dawson and they were frequently in the headlines. The Koyukuk country, over on the Alaska side of the line, was also much in the news just then, but fortunately and so far as the Stroller knows there was never a King of the Koyukuk. Even more fortunately, the Ku Klux Klan never became active in either the Klondike or the Koyukuk.

Fires and the Dawson Police Court furnished a good deal of local news, as the Stroller has previously mentioned, and another prolific source of copy was the Dawson theaters, of which there were several. There was lively competition among both the owners of the theaters and the actors and performers who appeared on their stages for newspaper space, and in that quarter at least the news reporters were esteemed and even respected. There were exceptions, however, and in such instances the reporters, although employed on rival papers and always eager to "scoop" the other fellows, stood together in upholding the dignity of their profession. Any ham-and-egg actor or actress who slighted a member of the Fourth Estate was at once taboo with the whole lot and usually was very soon minus an engagement as well.

But entertainers who were known as good scouts and who were inclined to "tote fair" with the reporters not only graced the front page frequently but received favorable stories under unfavorable circumstances. For example, if Cad Wilson or Nellie Holgate (who became the model for Rex Beach's Cherry Mellott) or any of the numerous footlight favorites became all bruised up as a result of falling down stairs or something — usually something — the reporters would explain that the bruises were caused by the gold nuggets which showered the bruisee when she responded to a third encore with "Just Tell Me That You Love Me and I Will Know the Rest." Or when Freddie Breen, a standby at the Standard Theatre, appeared on the stage thoroughly spiflicated and incapacitated in half a dozen other ways and was greeted with groans, the news stories told how the inimitable comedian had so perfectly impersonated a Rube actor that many in the audience were taken in and believed it was natural instead of put on.

But "Cecil Marian essayed to sing" was as good as Cecil was accorded in any of the papers; not that she was a poor singer but because she had cultivated an uppish attitude towards news reporters. Bessie Chandon carried a violin under her arm all the way from San Francisco to Dawson and her coming was widely and loudly heralded. But she snubbed the newsmen and after her first appearance the papers agreed that "Miss Chandon is not a violinist, or even a promising violin pupil."

It was reported in the papers as a happy social event when Fred Maurettis, a low comedian, fat and good-natured, assumed the garb of a priest and united Jim Hall and one of the Drummond sisters in fake bonds of matrimony. Jim, believing the rite to be the genuine article, presented his supposed bride with two thousand dollars in cash and everybody drank to their happiness in Mumm's Extra Dry at $25 a quart — at Jim's expense. What Jim said two days later when he came to was never printed. But the papers came to Jim's aid some months later when a number of his friends made an affidavit that he was of unsound mind in order to prevent him securing a license to wed Grace Anderson whose specialty was a barefoot dance. Perhaps the papers should have stayed out of it, but in consequence of their action the license was issued and they were married. Jim, who had cleaned up something like a million dollars on Eldorado Creek, purchased the Auditorium Theatre and gave it to Grace as a wedding present and they lived happily for a month, maybe six weeks. But right or wrong, the marriage and the bride's subsequent venture into the theatrical field as a manager were grist for the newsmill and made interesting copy, and that was what was essential to the papers if they were not to appear with blank pages.

Ranking as an equal of the theater as a news source was politics, especially municipal and territorial politics, since Dawson was too far from Ottawa to take much interest in Dominion affairs except on such occasions as Ottawa meddled with Dawson affairs. It was in 1901 that the Yukon Territorial Council delegated to Dawson the authority to form a municipal government and this she proceeded to do by electing a mayor and seven city councilmen. The initial meeting of the new council was something of an eye-opener to the electorate, for its first act was to vote an annual salary of $5,000 for the mayor and $3,600 for each of the councilmen, while a young lawyer who had boosted for the winning ticket was named city attorney, also at $3,600 a year.

One result of this action was to make seats on the aldermanic board much sought after, and each spring thereafter brought forth from twenty-five to forty candidates, all of them willing to sacrifice themselves pro bono publico. It happened that five of the seven members of the first Dawson City Council lived on Third Street, and by a majority vote of the council they decided to macadamize that street. This not only made it the most valuable business location in town but enhanced the value of abutting property, and the Stroller came close to being lynched for referring to it in a news story as "Aldermanic Avenue." But the Stroller desisted when the post of Official Reporter was created for him with emoluments, hereditaments and appurtenances nearly equal to the salary of the mayor.

Territorial political conventions in the Yukon were always lively affairs and the Stroller vividly recalls one held at the town of Caribou, which was on Dominion Creek. Just why it was held there, the Stroller does not know, as Caribou was forty-five miles from Dawson and about the same distance from any given point, and the only way to reach it was by a stage which scaled the dizzy dome separating Hunker and Dominion Creeks, at $20 per scale. The convention met in the Gold Belt Hotel, a place which fitted the description Sam Dunham gave the late Ed Levante's roadhouse at Eagle:

> The latchstring always hung outside
> And you didn't have to knock;
> He had no knocker on the door
> And he hadn't any lock.
> But when you ordered porterhouse
> He dished up caribou,
> And when you craved a whiskey straight
> He served you hoochinoo.

The landlord at the Gold Belt Hotel was handicapped by having lost his bartender the day before the convention opened, but he was fortunately able to enlist the services of a neighbor and the convention was able to proceed. This neighbor had a place of business across the street from the hotel, advertised by a sign which read UNDERTAKING, EMBALMING & ICE CREAM PARLOR but he did well enough as a bartender, or at least a bartender for a political convention.

The convention, which lasted for three days and would have lasted longer but that the delegates needed sleep, was what was termed a howling success; at any rate, there was a great deal of howling. The caliber of the delegates may be indicated by a brief but impassioned speech made by one of them who opposed a resolution favoring a miners' lien law.

"Lean law," he shouted. "Wat'sa matter you fellows? What's this here country coming to, anyway? We don't need no lean law for miners. Make 'em stand up straight!"

The convention broke up in a row with an assortment of black eyes and general contusions and every candidate nominated by it was defeated in the election six weeks later. It may have been the convention, too, that put the kibosh on the town of Caribou, which went into a decline shortly afterward and never recovered, although it was in the center of a busy mining district. The next time the Stroller saw the place, while nestled in a fur robe as he passed through on the stage the following winter, owls were hooting in the garret of the Gold Belt Hotel and the services of the embalmer-ice cream vendor were no longer in demand.

But although Caribou wasted away and finally disappeared, Dawson remained lively and continued to grow and that was where most of the news-gathering centered. Even in Dawson, however, there were times when fires were few, court cases became dull and routine, the theater went stale and politics was dormant. At such times the reporters fell back on that old stand-by, the personal interview. And a favorite subject, when a reporter had a couple of columns to fill and not much of anything to put in them, was a man known as Captain Jinks. He was always available; at times, in fact, he was over-available. But what really endeared him to the reporters was the fact that he did not give two whoops whether he was quoted correctly or incorrectly so long as he was quoted and his name was displayed prominently.

Captain Jinks did not mine gold, sell goods, tend bar, deal cards, spin a roulette wheel or follow any of the other occupations common to Dawson in that day, and how he managed to live was something of a mystery although there were rumors of a regular remittance from somewhere Back East. But he did live, and fairly well, too, and he occupied himself by being a chairman. He was a natural-born chairman and he followed that calling faithfully, with time out only for newspaper interviews. Whenever the occasion required a chairman, Captain Jinks was on hand for the job, and if the occasion did not arise frequently enough to suit him, he assisted in churning them up.

It was a rare day when the governor of Yukon Territory was not visited by a delegation seeking something or other. Many wrongs, most of them imaginary, existed and required righting: the price of miners' licenses was too high; fees for recording claims were exorbitant; it was a shame the way the gamblers were lined up every thirty days and fined $50 and costs; Uncle Hoffman was charging forty percent a month on loans to members of the perfesh, and so forth. All of these things and many others were called to the attention of the governor by delegations which were invariably headed by Captain Jinks. And before, after and between such calls, Captain Jinks was available, and eager, for interviews by the reporters.

He was a boon to the news reporters in another way, too, as he was always the chairman of meetings pertaining to schools, hospitals and other civic affairs. From the point of view of the reporters he was a good chairman because he never called anybody to order and never did anything to quiet the disturbances which usually arose at such meetings. A meeting that did not develop at least one good fist fight was considered a total loss by the reporters, but there were few such losses when Captain Jinks presided. And to top off his sterling qualities, he was religiously inclined; so much so that he never took a drink, except for his stomach's sake. But his stomach required much attention and he was never known to refuse something for its sake; it made a demand every time there was anything in sight, which in those days in Dawson was very frequently.

At times when Captain Jinks' stomach treatments incapacitated him temporarily and other news was scarce, the reporters were thrown upon their own resources of imagination and ingenuity, and the results were sometimes astounding. There was, for example, the time the cold weather turned a large quantity of liquor to water. The facts were simple: In the fall of 1899 a shipment of liquor valued at about $30,000 was caught by the ice and frozen in about a hundred miles up the river from Dawson. A watchman was placed in charge and it remained there all winter. When navigation opened in the spring the shipment was delivered to the consignees at Dawson, but when the casks were opened they contained water and nothing but water.

Ordinarily this would not have been worth more than a paragraph in the papers, but times were dull and the reporters blew it up into a marvel unrivaled since the Biblical water into wine stunt. The facts were examined from every possible angle and there were long and involved explanations, all of them allegedly scientific. Opinion was solicited from many sources as to whether the change had been gradual or whether it had occurred all at once when the temperature dropped to a certain point, and whether the whiskey, rum and brandy had all turned at the same temperature. All in all, it made a fine, paper-selling series of stories and only one pertinent fact was omitted. The reporters neglected to mention that there was a well-traveled dog sled trail between the liquor cache and Dawson, and that this trail, far from straight to begin with, had grown more and more crooked as the winter progressed.

NOSEY

I⊤ WAS DURING his earliest days in the new and mushrooming town of Skagway, and while he was still attempting to ferret out its best sources for news items, that the Stroller first ran into the most prolific fountain of news the town possessed. In fact, the Stroller does not hesitate to say that this fellow was the greatest hound for news he has ever come across in an experience that has ranged from the Everglades of Florida to within the shadow of the Pole. To the news reporters of Skagway, and later of Dawson, the fellow was manna in the wilderness. If there was any news floating around, that fellow corralled it, and if he didn't have any in stock, he manufactured it. He was good for a column every day of the week.

The fellow, who went by the name of Harry, was not a professional gatherer of news and had never written a line of copy in his life. He was, in fact, a bartender, and from all appearances he was no better than a rough hand at that trade. The Stroller does not know just where Harry ranked in Skagway's rather complicated social scale for bartenders, but he estimates that while Harry may have been a little below a high-class bartender, he was considerably above the lowest grade, which meant that the cash drawer at least broke even when he was on shift. Presumably Harry also had another name, but the Stroller does not remember what it was, if he ever heard it, and Harry was generally known as "Harry at the Nugget" or "Harry at the Merchant's," or whatever the name of the saloon where he was currently employed happened to be. He was also known, for reasons that will presently appear, as Wipe

'Em Up Harry, but the news reporters and editors knew him among themselves simply as Nosey, a name that was not, under the circumstances, intended to imply criticism but was wholly descriptive.

Nosey did his news gathering only while he was on shift behind a bar, which was twelve hours out of each twenty-four, but during that time he worked at it assiduously. Any time two or more customers engaged in private conversation at the bar, that particular section of the bar at once required wiping and polishing and Nosey approached it with towel in hand and a guileless expression on his face. Never did anyone eavesdrop more avidly or with more apparent disinterest than Nosey. And while his busy towel gained him the nickname Wipe 'Em Up, few if any of the customers ever became aware of the real purpose of the towel.

It was not an uncommon practice, of course,for bartenders to pick up bits of information from one customer and pass them on to the next, and many of them considered it to be a part of their regular duties. But the information thus traded was ordinarily that given them freely by the customers and for the most part it was useless to the news reporters for it had been so widely circulated that it was worn thin by the time it could be put into print. But Nosey was different. While he soaked up secrets like a sponge, he yielded not a one until a news reporter happened along. Then the floodgates opened and the reporter got information faster than he could jot it down. Nosey never asked for anything in return and the only string he attached was: "Don't say where you got it." And since little was sacred to the newspapers of that day, startling items of news were published and a great many secrets became public property as a result of Nosey's talents and his employment of them.

Some of the people involved must have stayed awake

nights wondering how their secrets got out, but the industrious bar-wiper was never suspected. His look of complete unconcern was adequate protection and in fact was so well maintained that he was often consulted on matters of business, matrimony and domestic affairs and this of course added to his stock in trade. An oracle of wisdom, he always knew when to say "no" to a customer, especially if the customer had already blown his last dime and wished for a nightcap or an eyeopener on the house. Nosey had one other quality, too, that was of great help to him behind the bar. He could look a woman straight in the eye and tell her he had not seen her husband for a week, and he could do this when the husband was at that moment crouching under the bar at Nosey's feet. Furthermore, he would solemnly inform the woman that if her husband happened to drop in he would be sent home at once. Nosey created such an impression of forthright honesty when he talked to wives that he was frequently invited to drop around some evening for dinner.

Both the Stroller and Nosey eventually landed in Dawson where they plied their respective trades and where the latter continued to be a right bower to the news reporters. Nosey so improved his natural faculties at Dawson that he could absorb three conversations at once and could do this without mixing up the facts oftener than about five times out of nine. Of course, it made no real difference to the reporters if he did mix them, for the stories were frequently more startling, caused more trouble and consequently sold more papers when the facts of a number of different conversations were mixed than when they were not.

One night when Nosey was on duty in Dawson a woman entered the saloon seeking her husband, and Nosey told her the old story about not having seen him for a week. But this time it happened to be true. And, relaxing his long-standing habit of keeping mum except to news reporters, Nosey further informed her that her husband had taken a boat to Whitehorse in company with Maude the Moose who had been doing a specialty number at the Orpheum, and that the pair of them were by then well on their way to Seattle. This unaccustomed candor was Nosey's undoing; before he quite realized what was happening the woman had divorced her husband and had Nosey before the alter where he murmured "I do" in a dazed but audible tone. She then persuaded him to quit tending bar and to buy a little grocery store, and surprisingly enough this business was prospering when the Stroller left Dawson a year or so later.

None of this would probably have come to the Stroller's mind had he not, one day last week, gone down to the dock while a southbound steamer was in port. And there on the dock, he encountered Nosey, the oldtime fountain of news whom he had not seen in more than twenty years. The Stroller naturally inquired how these fleeting years had dealt with his old friend, although to judge from his old friend's appearance he had been dealt to from the bottom of the deck, and perhaps a stacked deck at that.

Nosey's story was neither long nor sweet. All had gone well until about a year previously when he had fallen ill and the doctor had advised an operation. Nosey and his wife sold the store, which had continued to prosper, for a good figure and Nosey entered the hospital. Tears welled in his faded but honest eyes as he related to the Stroller that he was no sooner under the anaesthetic than his wife copped their entire roll and headed south, leaving only a note saying that she was going to join No. 1 who had shucked Maude somewhere along the road and was now running a greasy spoon joint in San Francisco. When he got out of the hospital, Nosey had clerked in his former store until he got enough money to pay the hospital bill

100

and buy a ticket for San Francisco where he hopes to recover his share of the roll. No. 1 is welcome to the woman, he said, if they will hand over half of what was received from the sale of the business in Dawson.

Having gotten this sad tale off his chest, Nosey brightened up and began to relate the story of a fellow passenger who had always been looked upon as an exemplary family man but who was certainly rolling 'em high on this trip. He had just reached the details of how high the man was rolling 'em when the steamer unfortunately blew her cast-off whistle and Nosey had to scramble aboard or be left behind.

As the steamer let go her lines and was backing away from the dock, the Stroller noticed a devoted-looking couple leaning against the rail and engaged in what seemed to be a very confidential conversation. And before they were out of sight, the Stroller noted that Nosey was there, too, and that he had pulled a handkerchief from his pocket and was vigorously wiping and polishing the rail as he edged closer and closer to the conversing couple.

CASEY
MORAN

A FEW DAYS AGO the Stroller received through the mail a copy of *The Tropical Sun,* a newspaper published in Maracaibo, Venezuela, and edited by his long-time friend and former associate, the loveable and irrepressible little Irishman, Bernard H. "Casey" Moran. As a result, the memory of the Stroller was wafted back to those years when Casey was in full and joyous bloom, both in Alaska and the Yukon.

Casey was born somewhere in California and grew up in Seattle where he was a newsboy and was known as the "Union Kid." It had nothing to do with the labor movement; rather, Casey had staked out Union Street as his territory, and woe be to any other newsboy who encroached on it. He was just about the hardest proposition in town when it came to a battle with his fists. But there was one thing all the boys said of "Casey" and that was, "Casey's straight." And his gold rule was, "Never paste a feller after he hollers 'Quit'."

Casey was not much past his twenty-first birthday when he landed in Juneau in the year 1895. At that time icebergs often drifted into the harbor at Juneau from Taku Glacier, and when Casey saw an iceberg he decided that opportunity was knocking at his door. He borrowed a rowboat, chipped off a hundred pounds or so of ice, and returned to town. Then he borrowed a wheelbarrow and peddled his ice around among the saloons, of which Juneau had more than just a few. Some of the money he cleared on this venture was invested in business cards which announced to the world:

B. H. "CASEY" MORAN
Wholesale and Retail Ice Dealer
Ice Supplied
By the Pound, Ton or Berg

In order to build his new business to successful proportions, Casey had to educate the population of Juneau to drink iced cocktails and use ice in their other refreshments, and he threw himself into this campaign with characteristic verve and energy. The campaign consisted mainly of buying samples of the novelty for any and all who would partake thereof, and it was successful. At the end of a few months, Casey was disposing of all the ice he could readily gather. But he was also in debt to every saloon in town for the sample drinks and he calculated he would have to supply free ice for four years to square himself, even if he signed the pledge himself and kept it. He opened a side line of bill posting, which was lucrative, but not lucrative enough.

About that time, in the late summer of 1896, the Post Office Department let a one-trip contract to carry a load of mail from Juneau to Circle City on the Yukon. Casey and Bill Ash of Juneau bid on and got the contract and were able to get to Circle City before the freeze-up.

Casey managed a minstrel show for the Miners Association, and for years afterward old-timers recalled it as the best minstrel show in the Interior up to that time. Leaving out the fact that it was probably also the first show of its kind in that part of the country, it evidently was a good one because Casey was rewarded with a nugget-studded gold ring which he greatly treasured.

Later that same winter Casey and most of the rest of the population of Circle City moved up the river to the Klondike where George Carmack had made his famed discovery the previous August.

103

Casey became a prospector and located a number of claims. One of them, on Sulphur Creek, proved very desirable and he secured a Crown grant to it. In the summer and fall of that year, 1897, the vanguard of the big Gold Rush reached the Klondike and Dawson sprouted, budded and burst into bloom. After that it was heavenly bliss, long drawn out, for Casey. Fearing that he might miss something, he burned his bed and slept, when he slept at all, under a crap table in one of the new gambling houses.

One afternoon up at the Forks Casey raked in $7,000 bucking the tiger and at once started down the trail to Dawson with visions of what he would do with the money. In telling a friend about it later, he said:

"I hit town at 9 o'clock that night and — by the way, did you ever hear of the howl in Rome?"

"I've heard that expression, yes."

"Well, it wasn't even a whisper compared to mine. I was broke by daylight!"

One night when Casey was dancing at the Monte Carlo, Humboldt Gates, who later became a brother-in-law of Senator Key Pittman of Nevada, called him off the floor and offered $20,000 for the claim on Sulphur Creek. Casey was agreeable and Gates asked him to step next door to the gambling room where the gold dust cashier would weigh out $2,000 to bind the bargain until morning, when the remaining $18,000 would be paid. But Casey laughed and wanted to know how a man could dance with ten pounds of gold dust in his pockets, and he turned down the offer and resumed the light fantastic.

The next morning Swiftwater Bill Gates — he was no relation to Humboldt Gates — asked Casey to make out a bill of sale to the claim on Sulphur and loan it to him so he could put it up as security for a grubstake. The Northern Commercial Company was always willing to advance grubstakes to the owners of promising claims. Casey was happy to oblige his friend Swiftwater and — well, Swiftwater was a little too swift for Casey, and Casey never recovered title to his property.

During the next year or so Casey worked in laundries, dealt faro, married a nice girl and did several other things before discovering that a talent for newspaper reporting lurked in his system. The Stroller well remembers the morning Casey came to work as his understudy. It was a Monday morning, and when Thursday evening's paper went to press, Casey had not been to bed since he took the job. He was afraid our "esteemed contemptuaries," as he designated the two rival dailies, would get a scoop on us. But when the paper went to press on Thursday evening Casey decided to take a cat nap and he crawled up on a high stack of newsprint and went to sleep. The office was somewhat wobbly on its foundations — posts had cost $16 apiece when it was built and had been used sparingly — and when the press got down to business it shook the building so that Casey rolled off his temporary bed and almost broke his neck. Then he went home and slept the rest of the week.

As a resourceful reporter, Casey Moran was a glowing success. He could dig up more news, and make a bigger mess of writing it up, than anyone the Stroller ever saw. In fact, the Stroller never had a silver thread in his raven locks until he began editing copy turned in by Casey.

But Casey demonstrated his flair for imaginative reporting, and gained lasting fame for himself at the same time, one winter morning when the temperature had dropped below the bottom of the thermometer. The telegraph line had been down for a week, there had been no mail for the best part of a month, and the people of Dawson were huddled up to keep warm and making no news that could be printed. Casey and the Stroller were hugging close to the big heater in the newspaper office that morning, trying to think up excuses for not going out to search for news, while the editor was tearing his hair and demanding something that would sell papers. Finally there was nothing to do but go, and Casey went one way while the Stroller headed in the other direction and toward the nearest saloon where there was a little warmth and where there just might possibly be a story.

When the Stroller returned a couple of hours later there was the glimmering of a fanciful tale about ice worms hovering in the back of his mind, and he found Casey already hard at work. Casey grunted that he "had something." While he was not generally given to understatement, that one was monumental. He "had something" indeed.

On that wintry morning, Casey had run across an Indian — a chief, of course; we never dealt with anything lower than a chief in the newspapers — and the Indian claimed to have discovered a "hiyu big canoe" on top of a mountain in the Koyukuk country of Alaska the previous summer. Moreover, the canoe had a big house on it "just like white man's house in town." Both the canoe and the house were very big and very, very old, so old, in fact, that the wood in them had turned to stone.

Casey hustled the Indian over the home of a minister who owned an illustrated Bible, and in that he found a picture of Noah's Ark. The picture, declared the Indian, was identical with the structure on the mountain top except for the evidences of age in the latter. Casey wrote out these facts in the form of an affidavit, got the Indian to make his mark at the bottom of it before witnesses, and had his story.

Such a story deserved top billing, and the Stroller got busy writing the headline while Casey put the finishing touches on the text. And the Stroller ran into difficulties at once, for while we had plenty of 72-point headline type, there were only three K's in the font and the Stroller was confronted with ARK and KOYUKUK in the same headline.

"Why couldn't you have put it on a mountain in the Tanana or the Chandalar or almost any other part of Alaska except the Koyukuk?" the Stroller growled at Casey.

"You wouldn't want me to make a liar out of that Indian, would you?" Casey responded innocently.

The Stroller first wrote:

RUINS OF NOAH'S BOAT
FOUND ON MOUNTAIN TOP
IN KOYUKUK COUNTRY

But that wouldn't do. The little steamboats that then plied the Yukon and its tributaries by the dozen were forever getting stranded or mislaid. Noah's Boat might have referred to almost any of them. After some more trial scribbling, the headline finally appeared:

RUINS OF NOAH'S ARK
FOUND ON MOUNTAIN
IN KOYUKUC COUNTRY

Even without its full quota of K's in the headline, the story was a sensation and the paper sold by the hundreds both in Dawson and out among the mining camps on the creeks. And when the telegraph line was repaired a few days later, the story went out to the waiting world where it likewise created astonishment and did considerable damage, temporarily at least, to the Mount Ararat tradition.

But if imaginative reporting was Casey's long suit, politics was his downfall. The winter of 1901-02 came on and with it three political campaigns. One was for the election of a member of the Dominion Parliament, another for the election of a member of the Yukon Council, and the third was to elect a mayor and several aldermen for the city of Dawson. Casey yearned to be in the midst of one of more of these campaigns, and as an active candidate, but since he was what was in Dawson designated as a d——d Yankee, he was handicapped.

One evening shortly before the deadline for candidates to file, Casey came into the newspaper office where the Stroller was at work and took a chair on the other side of the table. He didn't say a word and this in itself was highly unusual. The Stroller could see that Casey had something on his mind, and he knew that Casey would not long contain whatever it was. Finally, Casey heaved a tumultuous sigh and blurted out:

"Well, I became a Canadian today."

Now, while the Stroller considers that Canadians are the salt of the earth, he could not see then or any other time why an American should foreswear allegiance to the Stars and Stripes to become a subject of the King or of anyone else. So he rather bluntly responded, "Casey, you poor fish!"

For the next five minutes the ticking of the silent watches of the night could be distinctly heard in that office. Then Casey arose without a word, donned his fur coat and drifted into the forty-below weather outside. Two hours later he returned, wearing a red plush jag and crying like a baby.

"Shay, why didn't you smash me right in the face?" he asked. "Why didn't you knock me down and stomp all over me? It wouldn't have hurt half as bad as what you said."

And when he returned to work a day or two later, Casey was greatly humbled and chastened in spirit. His wife was from Alabama and from what Casey told the Stroller, she had poured out vials of wrath such as are only produced in the South and she had poured them with a heavy hand distinctly characteristic of outraged southern womanhood. She had started with, "Sah, I thought I had married a man of honor, and I find ah'm married to a jellyfish," and had gone on from there.

Nevertheless, Casey filed for a seat on the aldermanic board, having been attracted to that position by the fact that the members had voted themselves salaries of $300 a month, and he threw himself into the campaign. He faced an uphill battle because his principal opponent in the contest was a saloon owner whose platform contained two planks:

1. Free whiskey.
2. Plenty of it.

But Casey worked hard, and ten days before the election he took a leave of absence from his newspaper job to devote full time to the campaign. As women then had the vote in Dawson, he gave them extra attention. He complimented them on their complexions, their youthful appearance, their clothes, their cooking, and everything else he could think of to compliment them on without getting his face slapped. He talked to every voter he could corner and methodically recorded, in a notebook he carried for that purpose, the name of each of them who promised to vote for him. In addition, he kissed all the babies in that end of the territory, distributed cigars, bought largely of a product of Scotland, and in many other ways demonstrated his capabilities as a politician.

On the day of the election, about the time the polls were to close, Casey dropped in at the newspaper office wearing a bright mantle of confidence. He displayed the notebook in which were recorded the names of 968 people who had promised him their vote, and he offered to bet $100 against $10 that he would lead the count by at least a hundred votes. No one called the bet.

"Yer a bunch of pikers, the whole lot of ye," he flung over his shoulder as he sailed out the door, slamming it behind him.

Several hours later he was back. The ballots had been counted and out of 1,288, Casey had received 47. He was heartbroken. "Tell me the truth," he sobbed. "What am I? I'm not an American any more. I swore allegiance to the King. I may be a whitewashed Canadian, but I'm not accepted by the Canadians. The votes prove that. Only forty-seven of the 968 who promised to vote for me kept the promise, and I don't even know which ones they are. Now, will you please tell me just what in hell I am?"

But Casey recovered. As the Stroller mentioned at the beginning of this story, he was irrepressible. Also, when Casey had something to say, he said it and it was usually straight to the point. The Stroller recalls the occasion of a funeral at Dawson at which Casey served as one of the pall-bearers. It was in the nightless part of summer and a prominent and influential gambler had died. Since he had been a nighthawk all his life and had, in fact, seldom seen the midday sun, his friends decided it would be appropriate to bury him at midnight. The graveside services were conducted by the minister of the Church of England, and they were lengthy indeed. The mosquitoes were out that night in force, and they were ravenous. Finally Casey could stand it no longer and from his place at a corner of the coffin he said, in a whisper that could be heard for at least a block: "Father, Father, can't you speed this thing up a little? The mosquitoes are eating us alive!"

Elmer John "Stroller" White. (Stroller White III Collection)

Clockwise from below: *A mountain in Juneau was named for Stroller a year after his death.* (Stroller's Weekly, October 30, 1931); *Stroller* (left) *was the Alaska territorial government's first director of publicity.* (Stroller White III Collection); *THE KLONDIKE NUGGET was the first newspaper Stroller toiled for in Dawson City.* (National Archives of Canada)

A WORTHY CITIZEN HONORED

When the National Geographic Board at its October meeting gave the name of "Mount Stroller White" to a prominent peak on the northwest side of Mendenhall gracier, some 15 miles from Juneau, it conferred a distinctive honor upon the memory of a worthy Juneau citizen and the dean of Northern newspapermen.

In thus honoring Mr. White every citizen of Alaska including the newspaper fraternity may rejoice that in honoring Mr. White the Geographic Board conferred a signal honor upon all Alaskans.

Too many of our rivers, lakes, bays, peaks and geographic locations are named after some English or Spanish explorer. They should be named after men who, like Mr. White, spent a long and useful life in attempting to place Alaska before the world.

Mr. E. J. White was one of the foremost journalists and newspaper men of the entire Northern empire. He lived continuously in the North for 33 years, and during that time saw his efforts come to near fruition. One of the most widely-known and widely-read men of both Territories, he made friends by the thousands, and kept them. Our friend of yesterday has passed on, but his memory has been perpetuated for the tomorrows.

If this paper can carry on with the calm determination and unfaltering loyalty to principles manifest in the writings of "Stroller White," we will feel that we have not worked in vain. It is impossible to emulate his teachings, but we can hew along the lines which have immortalized his name.

Sour Dough Hotel

1333 ICICLE AVENUE

Best House North of Mexico.   First-class in Every Particular.
Rates; One Ounce per Day.

Crap, Chuck Luck, Stud Poker and Black Jack Games Run by the Management

Private Entrance for Ladies by Ladder in the Rear. Special Rates for Ministers and the Gambling "Perfesh" Every Known Fluid—Water Excepted—For Sale at the Bar Dogs Bought and Sold. Insect Powder for sale at the Bar.

☞ Not responsible for diamonds, bicycles or other valuables kept under the pillows; they should be deposited in the safe.
If you are fond of athletics and like good jumping, lift the mattress and see the bed spring.

Broadway, Skagway, Alaska - May, 1898

HOUSE RULES

Towels changed weekly.
Dogs not allowed in the bunks.
Candles and Hot Water charged extra.
Board $2.00 per square foot. Meals extra.
Spiked boots must be removed at night.
Guests are requested not to speak to the Dumb Waiter.
Anyone troubled with nightmare will find a halter on the bed-post.
If the room gets too warm, open the window anl see the fire escape.
Base-ballists desiring a little practice will find a pitcher on the stand.
Don't worry about paying your bill; the house is supported by its foundations.
The hotel is convenient to all cemeteries. Hearses for fire at 25 cents a second.
Guests wishing to do a little driving will find hammer and nails in the closet.
Guests wishing to get up without being called can have self-rising flour for supper.
If the lamp goes out, take a feather out of the pillow; that's light enough for any room.

Clockwise from below: *Skagway's famous "Little Egypt" cast spells on many would-be miners.* (Yukon Archives); *Skagway teemed with activity in May, 1898 at the time the Stroller arrived. The Skagway News sign can be seen behind the power pole to the left, pointing to the office in the alley.* (Dedman's Photo Shop); *Stroller probably had something to do with the advertisement and house rules for the "Sourdough Hotel."* (Stroller White III Collection)

Clockwise from below: *The Monogram was a typical Skagway watering hole, where the Stroller trained bartenders to "put a squirt of lemon in it."* (Yukon Archives); *Stroller's son, Albert,* (ctr.) *and his friends mush dogs on the streets of Whitehorse.* (Stroller White III Collection); *As many as four wharfs stuck out from Skagway like fingers ready to grab the unwitting stampeders off the steamships* (Yukon Archives).

Clockwise from above: *Jody White, Stroller's wife.* (Stroller White III Collection); *The classy Pack Train Restaurant was the Stroller's favorite Skagway eatery* (Alaska Historical Library); *Stroller, late in life, outside his home in Douglas.* (Stroller White III Collection); *Lenore White, Stroller's daughter.* (Stroller White III Collection)

When he left Dawson, Casey went to Fairbanks where he added to his fame as a reporter. He then moved on to Seattle and worked for a couple of daily papers, and for a time he was in New York on the staff of *Collier's Weekly*.

He joined the rush to the Cobalt country in northern Canada where he operated a small paper, and from there he went to California and sold oil stock, then drifted down to Mexico and published a paper in Monterrey. Later he was in Columbia and in Venezuela, where he is today.

A few years ago there was a report from South America that Casey Moran had died there, but before long Casey himself contradicted the report. Meanwhile, however, shaken with grief, the Stroller wrote that "Casey Moran was one of God's noblemen and his death will cast a mantle of gloom over what Robert Service calls 'The Brotherhood of Men Who Know the North'." On the whole, the Stroller gave Casey a much better write-up at that time than he will probably ever get again.

But looking back now, the Stroller sees no reason to retract those words, premature though they may have been. Just as there was only one Klondike, there was only one Casey Moran, and the two complemented each other. There can never be another pair like them. But while the Klondike has faded in all but memory, Casey Moran continues to dispense the sunshine from his great Irish heart through the medium of his newspaper, and the Stroller hopes that he will continue to do so for many years to come.

[Compiler's note: Bernard H. "Casey" Moran outlived Stroller White by approximately three years. He died at Maracaibo, Venezuela, on November 22, 1933.]

THE ICE WORM STORY

THE NORTHLAND is thundering down the corridors of Time without a distinctive and personal class of literature. There have been meters, furlongs and miles of writing about Alaska and the Yukon, and much of it, especially the meters, has been wholly devoid of metre or much of anything else save words — a multiplicity of words. What is needed is something in the way of literature on which the brand of the North is so defined and distinctive that it may not be mistaken. That there is much in the North to inspire high class writing is beyond question, but with very few exceptions the writers who could produce such literature have never been accorded the encouragement their efforts deserved.

Back in the early and glorious years when the words "Alaska" and "Klondike" were heralded from the river unto the ends of the earth, hundreds of writers and would-be writers invaded the Northland. Some of them brought talent, while many brought nothing except the clothes in which they stood. But they came from all corners of the globe, bringing letters of introduction from Lord Strathcona or the editor of the Prune Growers' Journal. They came singly and in pairs and flocks, male and female, young, middling and superannuated. Many of them had never actually written a line for publication in their lives. Others were never sober if they could beg, borrow or purloin the price to be otherwise, and in those free and easy days they were generally otherwise.

The Stroller remembers as fairly typical of the lot a man who came from London and wrote a large part of the alphabet after his name. He had a two-storey forehead, carried seventeen lead pencils, and talked learnedly of telepathic communications which came to him direct from Mother Nature every time he took a sneak into the brush where there was naught to disturb the telepathic intake. It was his announced intention to write short stories and market them locally to meet his temporal needs, meanwhile corralling the information for a book that would revolutionize the literature of Christendom. His theory may have been sound, but it fell down when he attempted to put it into practice. The market for the kind of stories he turned out was very bearish around Dawson, and before long there came demand from the region below his belt for nourishment, demands that refused to lie low. The result was a triumph of matter over mind and he got a job as a dishwasher at the Silver Tip Cafe and his literary life washed down the drain with the soapsuds.

The hundreds of writers who came north at that time had two things in common. They were all intent upon giving to the Northland a kind of literature that would stand out through the ages as though carved on the azure dome of heaven and painted red. And they would all look offended if you did not invite them over to the Dutchman's to have something, at four-bits per something.

Their intentions were noble, but nothing much ever came of them. The male contingent was absorbed in one way or another, most of it finding employment in menial positions such as reporters on newspapers, cuspidor wrestlers in the saloons, or boosters at the blackjack tables. And the women, bless 'em, mostly married miners or

113

prospectors and were led from the alter to the washtub, where their literary aspirations evaporated in the steam or faded out with the dye in the denims.

The Stroller, in his own meek and cow-eyed manner, once made an attempt to inflict some distinctly northern literature on the unsuspecting world, and for a time he congratulated himself that he had succeeded. It happened this way:

It was a cold winter morning in Dawson and the newspaper business was at a very low ebb. There had been no mail for nearly a month and the telegraph line had been out of commission for more than a week. In consequence, no news was forthcoming from the great world outside, while local news was scarce as to quantity and insipid as to quality. The editor was pacing the office and alternately moaning and tearing his hair. The paper, he announced, had reached bedrock; the only way it could sink lower would be to fold up and go out of business entirely.

"Go out and rustle up some news," he demanded. "Get me something that will make headlines and sell papers."

The Stroller and Casey Moran had been hovering around the office stove all morning and churning their brains for excuses to remain there, for the temperature outdoors had dropped to seventy degrees below zero, Fahrenheit.

"You call yourselves reporters," the editor stormed. "Why an old squaw with a rusty nail and piece of board could write a better story than the two of you today. Now get out!"

It was apparent that the temperature of the editor had reached 212 degrees above zero, Fahrenheit, and since he was known to have a flash point of 213 degrees, Casey and the Stroller scrambled into their parkas and got.

Casey wandered off into the ice fog and eventually returned with his justly famed contribution to archaeology, the discovery of Noah's Ark on a mountain top in Alaska. The Stroller headed for Tom Chisholm's Aurora Saloon. This was the one known as the big Aurora, for Tom had five other Auroras, six in all, the big Aurora being in Dawson and the five little Auroras out on the creeks where the miners worked. Tom believed in going after trade, and he got it. One reason for his success in getting trade was that he encouraged his customers to run accounts, and as the trade did not need much encouragement along that line, he soon built up a wonderful business. Of course, Tom eventually went broke, but that did not worry the trade. He still had the accounts, didn't he?

But all of that came later, and on this particular morning the trade at the Aurora, both cash and on account, was very slow. On more than one occasion the Stroller had received inspiration while rubbing the fine brass rail in the Aurora with the sole of his boot, but on this morning, although he rubbed and rubbed, nothing came of it. Nor did anything come of the inspiring beverage carefully poured for him by Tom's kindly bartender, who did not neglect the squirt of lemon. The Stroller next tried Bill McPhee's Northern and then Sam Bonnifield's Bank Saloon, but the brass rails there were no more productive and at last he could no longer postpone his return to the newspaper office.

As the Stroller trudged along the deserted Dawson street that morning, empty-handed and empty-headed, he heard somewhere behind him in the ice fog the squeak, squeak, squeak of a sled runner on the dry and powdery snow. And that sound gave him a faint glimmering of an idea. So, after Casey's Ark story had been polished up and a headline composed for it, the Stroller got busy on filling his own allotted space. He wrote a simple and straightforward story in which he reported that the extremely low temperatures had combined with the recent heavy fall of blue snow to bring thousands and thousands of ice worms out of their beds in the glaciers surrounding Dawson to bask in the frigidity. They had crawled forth in such numbers, in fact, that their chirping was keeping the people of Dawson awake nights, and if the temperature did not rise soon to send the ice worms back into cold storage, something drastic would have to be done.

Casey's Noah's Ark story was a sensation and the Stroller's story made something of a hit as he realized the following day when he entered the Northern Saloon and saw a large placard which read: "Ice Worm Cocktails, $1." The bartender spotted the Stroller at about the same moment and beckoned him closer.

"Better try one," said the bartender. "It's on the house."

While a crowd gathered to watch, the bartender carefully lifted the cover from a bowl of the finest cut glass, and there, embedded in a chunk of ice, were the ice worms, white and succulent. The bartender chipped off a piece of the ice and with a pair of silver tongs delicately drew forth one of the luscious creatures. He dropped it into a tall glass along with the ice and added other suitable ingredients.

As the bartender handed the glass to the Stroller, he drew close and whispered anxiously, "We couldn't catch any of the real thing so we had to fake 'em. We made holes in the ice with a gimlet, poked spaghetti in the holes and let it swell. Think they'll pass for the real thing?"

The Stroller tasted, smacked his lips and pronounced it the finest ice worm cocktail it had ever been his pleasure to imbibe. "Be sure always to use the youngest and freshest ice worms you can get," he advised the bartender. "Their bouquet when infants is superb." And during the remainder of the day the gentleman in the white coat could scarcely build ice worm cocktails fast enough to satisfy the demand.

The Stroller's little story was reprinted in other papers both in this country and abroad and brought a great response. The Scientific Research Society in London asked for details on the habits and environment of the ice worm and requested that specimens be forwarded by mail. The Department of Agriculture in Washington, D.C., wrote to the Stroller for further information on the creatures, and this was gladly furnished, free of charge and suitably embellished in keeping with the dignity of the department seeking it. The Stroller gloried in his position as the world's foremost authority on the ice worms.

Then some smart aleck of a writer employed by the *Philadelphia Ledger* butted in and got the Stroller in bad with the Department of Agriculture by reprinting the original story and following it with these lines:

Oh, liar, we adore thee
In humble awe
And pray that heaven bless thee
With tardy thaw.
Blue snow we all admire
But seldom see;
For news of it, Oh, liar,
We turn to thee.
Our ice worms, too, are dumb;
No chirp have they;
But in our ice are some
Bad germs, I say.
To Yukon, land august
Where zeros burn,
The local liar must
With envy turn.

Talk about being squelched, cast down and mortified! The Stroller was so deeply wounded that despite the fact that the Northland literally exudes inspiring subjects and opportunities, he has never since attempted to elevate its literature from the slime-covered slough of mediocrity in which it reposes.

Liar indeed! The Stroller will take his oath, now or any other time, that never has he seen blue snow or heard an iceworm chirp when the thermometer stood above seventy degrees below zero, Fahrenheit.

THE
EGGS
OF
DAWSON

EGGS PLAYED a prominent part in the early history of Dawson, and many of Dawson's eggs were famous in their own right — a right they acquired strictly by seniority. One of the distinguishing marks of a person who was a resident of Dawson during her ebullient days is that he never orders poached eggs. He lost the habit in Dawson, for eggs that would poach never reached that part of the country. Those were the days when eggs were eggs, and any that were under eight months old and would fry without getting up and climbing out of the skillet were rated as "Fresh" and found ready sale at $5 per dozen. Eggs that were closer to the chirping stage were labeled "For Cooking" and sold at only $4 per dozen. Chirpers were utilized mostly by restaurants that specialized in chicken soup. Boiling an egg in Dawson prior to about 1902 was prohibited by territorial law, the passing of which was brought about through the efforts of the Society for the Prevention of Cruelty to Animals, chickens being catalogued as animals as a matter of convenience.

A liking for the so-called "fresh" eggs of Dawson was distinctly an acquired taste and one that sometimes took a good deal of time to acquire. But once acquired, it also took considerable time to eradicate it, and a Dawsonite who went Outside where there were really fresh eggs was apt to complain that they were all flat and insipid. It was not at all unusual in Seattle and Vancouver, B.C., during the winter months to see a man wandering from one restaurant to another in search of some eggs with a flavor. He was almost invariably a Dawsonite.

One particular case of eggs, of the vintage of '97, was on exhibit for many years, beneath a hermetically sealed glass case, in the Territorial Museum at Dawson. Those were the very same eggs that Swiftwater Bill Gates paid one dollar per egg for at a time when it was the only case of eggs within a radius of four hundred miles and when Gussie Lamore was possessed of the greatest appetite for eggs within a radius of eight hundred miles.

Swiftwater was desirous of winning the heart and hand of the egg-loving Gussie, but the winsome Gussie was not to be wooed with eggs, especially eggs that had been in warm storage for many months. Fresh eggs would have been different, but Gussie knew eggs when she saw them or heard them coming, so she spurned Swiftwater and his eggs and told him to wait a few years and maybe her mother would be a widow, as her father had fallen arches and fatty degeneration and was liable to kick off at any time.

Swiftwater then vowed that he would eat those eggs or die in the attempt. He ate one, and was never the same afterward. For awhile he kept the eggs under the bed in his room, but every now and again one of the eggs would tender its resignation with a muffled report and there would be a complaint to the medical health officer. The eggs were finally sealed up in the glass container above mentioned and when Swiftwater left the Yukon he presented them to the museum where they were displayed in a place of honor between the Silver Dollar shovel that unearthed the first gold on Bonanza Creek and what was left of a pair of moccasins in which Nellie Cashman mushed out from the Koyukuk after having been the first white woman ever seen there.

During the months of summer, eggs arrived at Dawson by river steamer, either down the river from Whitehorse at the head of navigation or up the river from St. Michael, near its mouth. The last of these summer eggs reached Dawson sometime in October and were placed in winter storage until they had been used up, or had blown up. Navigation did not again open until late in May or early in June and it became the custom of the egg-importers to freight several loads of eggs over the winter trail before the spring break-up. Usually these egg-laden sleds began to arrive in Dawson early in April after having travelled some four hundred miles over the frozen bosom of the Yukon River. The importers sold the eggs to merchants at $90 to $100 per case, or $3 and up per dozen, and what the retailers got over and above that was their profit. But the first sled load of eggs each spring usually commanded even higher prices. The demand was so great that the owners auctioned them off to the highest bidders and the consumers ate $6 eggs, if they ate eggs at all. Many of them didn't.

The driver of the first egg sled to arrive at Dawson in the spring was something of a local celebrity for a few days and at the very least got his name and an interview in the papers. And in that connection the Stroller well remembers the arrival of the vanguard of the egg sleds in the spring of 1900. It resulted in a celebrated local murder case in which a Dawson newspaper reporter was arraigned on a charge that he had shot and killed the driver of the sled.

British justice is proverbial for being both swift and sure, and the accused man was placed on trial, on the day following the killing, before an austere-appearing judge arrayed in black judicial ermine. The jury was composed mostly of men who had the appearance of being hungry for eggs but whose means would permit them to indulge only in the near-chirping variety.

The Crown Prosecutor opened the case with a lengthy address embellished by quotations from many authorities, but which all boiled down to a declaration that the prisoner in the dock was guilty of cold-blooded murder. The Prosecutor added that he hoped the case would not occupy more than one day. The prisoner had no attorney and replied in the negative when asked if he wanted one. All he wanted, he said, was the privilege of telling the story of the shooting and the events leading up to it.

Many witnesses were called by the Crown, but none had actually seen the shooting, which had taken place in the office of the news reporter. No one had heard any quarrel or any loud talk, and not until the fatal shot rang out did anyone realize that a tragedy was imminent.

The Crown Prosecutor was eloquent but brief when he again addressed the jury. It was an open and shut case, he said, and the way he said it made the reporter's future appear very dark indeed.

His Lordship, the judge, informed the prisoner that he would be permitted to speak on his own behalf, but he asked that it be made brief. His Lordship, it seemed, had a pressing dinner engagement. The prisoner rose in the box.

"May it please your Lordship," he began. "The deceased came to me with an account of his somewhat strenuous trip down the congealed surface of the Yukon River as the driver of an egg-laden sled. Scenting a story for the paper by which I am employed, I encouraged the driver to give me details of the trip which lasted a total of twenty-six days. He did so. He told me of the cold he endured and how he was threatened by snow-blindness as a result of the glare of the sun reflected by the ice and snow. He related how he had to keep oil lanterns burning under the tarpaulin to prevent the freezing of the precious cargo of eggs. He added many other interesting and instructive items concerning the business of freighting eggs. Some of these things I already knew, but they were interesting and I could make use of them in my story. In consequence, I felt very kindly toward the man.

"But instead of concluding his story when he should have, he continued it. Looking me straight in the eye, he described how he had made the mistake of using a single case of eggs as a seat during the entire early part of the journey. Without a sign of flinching, he told me that after twenty-one days the entire case of eggs had hatched and that from that date on he had 360 young Shanghais and Plymouth Rocks to care for in addition to his task of keeping the remaining eggs from freezing.

"Your Lordship, I could have stood for this obvious prevarication, although it did destroy some of the friendly feeling I felt toward the man. But that was not the end. He edged close to the door, turned and said with a smirk: "I consider, without eggsageration, that I have had a most eggstraordinary eggsperience.'

"I could stand no more, Your Lordship. I saw red. I shot him. That is my sole defense."

"The jury will return a verdict of justifiable homicide," calmly announced the court. "Society must be protected. And the Prosecutor will please refrain in the future from taking the time of this court with such trivial cases. The court is adjourned."

His Lordship and the late prisoner walked up the street together. The latter "bought," and a friendship was born that has not since been obliterated by time or dimmed by separation.

GUSSIE
LAMORE

RECENTLY THERE floated into the Stroller's memory, from one of its deeper recesses, of which there is an ample supply, the name Gussie Lamore, a name from the distant past when the Northland bloomed and every dance hall had its covey of young and winsome women. Gussie was one of the earliest arrivals in Dawson after George Carmack stumbled onto the pay. Gussie and one of her several sisters — it may have been Grace — first came north to Juneau in the spring of 1896 with the Richard Maurettus Vaudeville Company. After playing at the Opera House in Juneau for a time, they went over the pass and down the Yukon to the booming camp of Circle City. That is where Gussie was when the Klondike was struck and she lost no time in getting up to the new camp.

The memory of the name sent the Stroller to scrabbling in the packing case full of ancient programs, bills-of-fare, scrawled notes and early newspaper clippings that constitutes his memoirs, and he came up with a handful of yellowed and fading clippings. One of them is this bit of immortal literature.

TO GUSSIE LAMORE

by Harry T. Munn

Ah, Gussie, my dear one, my dear one, my passionate, petulent pet!
In the anguish and grief of our parting, I have wished that we never had met.

Yet I would not have missed the sweet pleasure, for the
    months of my sorrowing pain;
To have kissed thee is joy beyond measure! Ah, when shall
    I kiss thee again?
With thy passionate farewell there lingers the scent of thy
    French Hill gold hair.
When the joy and the pain of thy presence paraded the
    nicotine air.
In thy eyes lay the love and the longing of Heaven's
    unspeakable blue,
And thy lips whispered soft words of warning as thy kisses
    were thrilling me through.
Yet, Gussie, don't misunderstand me. Don't grieve for your
    lover who's gone.
The sorrow of parting is over, the joy of our meeting's to
    come.
Make them order the wine by the dozen, in the boxes or up
    to your room;
Let the theater resound with their laughter! Sing them,
    Circe, to their ultimate doom.
Let the miners blow in all their gold dust; make them drink
    till they're full to the neck.
But, remember, the percentages must cash in with the
    usual check.
When — ah, curses! — they dare to enfold thee, when your
    lips with their kisses are wet,
Remember the things I have told thee — take their nuggets,
    take all you can get.
I am playing the races in 'Frisco, I am bucking the bank
    every night,
And to New York and Paris I am going, and yet I am still
    flying light.
So send me some nuggets and some of your jewels; you can
    get them replaced any time.
Your lovers are asinine donkeys — blow them in, take
    them all down the line!
Gussie Lamore! Hear them calling the queen of the Klondike
    in song.
When your nightingale notes have been thralling the crowd
    who have waited so long,

Perhaps if you offer a bit extra, the manager surely would
   see
It was worth twenty-five more on pay day, and that you
   could send on to me.
And some day — dear one, make it quickly — on shores
   that are kinder than these,
We will roam where the shadows lie thickly, 'mid the
   scented ambrosial trees,
Hand in hand down the glen we shall wander, in the haunt
   of the dove and the hare;
So be careful, my darling, don't squander — send me every
   cent you can spare.
Oh, my love! Oh, my golden-haired fairy, in the days
   which are yet to be born,
We shall roam o'er the earth's fairest places, your cheek
   laid to mine in the dawn;
Lip to lip, in sweet long-drawn embraces, surely never can
   we have enough;
So work on, my darling, like blazes, and send me the bulk
   of your stuff.

According to the date on the yellowed clipping, it was published in *The Klondike Nugget,* that joyous paper upon which the Stroller toiled for more than four years, on February 8, 1900, but it had been written the previous summer aboard the steamboat "Columbian".

The Stroller did not know Harry Munn in 1899 and he has not met him since. Nor does he desire to meet him. The Klondike, when it was in bloom, had too many of the kind who did not sow and neither did they reap except the earnings of the unfortunate young women who were sometimes known as fairies and sometimes by other terms the Stroller will not repeat here.

The Lamore sisters were very much a part of the night life of Dawson and so were often in the news. Now and then the Stroller had occasion to write something about the Lamores in the department called The Stroller that appeared regularly in *The Klondike Nugget*. The sisters also had a brother — at least, they said he was their brother — who went by the name Busch and who had a vaudeville turn that included walking a tight wire.

This story appeared in August, 1899: "Busch, the aerialist, and two of his sisters, Nellie and Gussie Lamore, took a sudden departure for San Francisco on Saturday and on inquiry it developed that they feared Nellie might be scheduled to play one part in a double tragedy such as the one last Friday when Maude Roselle, an actress at the Monte Carlo, was shot and killed by Harry Davis, who then put a bullet in his own brain. Nellie hasn't enjoyed life long enough, however, and as she is believed to have a good big roll of the long green saved up, she was open to the suggestion that a trip below would be beneficial."

Gussie, at least, did not stay away from Dawson very long because in October of that same year this item appeared in the column written by the Stroller:

There was a hot old time in the Opera House during the early hours of Wednesday. "Hooch," a well-known faro dealer, showed too much partiality for "Cigarette Lizzie,' whom he treated so liberally and so often that the envy of Gussie Lamore and Lucy Lovell was aroused. Gussie freely expressed her opinion respecting Lizzie's character, and the latter retaliated by classing the fair Gussie among the feline species. A fast and furious physical contest immediately resulted. The erstwhile wife of Swiftwater Bill attempted to scratch and claw, but Lizzie countered with a couple of stiff left arm jabs which landed on Gussie's optic. The fracas was at the point of assuming serious proportions when a cry of "Police"restored peace and order and almost sobriety among the contestants.

Another of the clippings from The Stroller department is dated in April, 1900:

Gussie Lamore succeeded in creating considerable diversion at the entertainment which was recently given at a local theater in honor of the Fraternal Order of Eagles. She assumed no part in the production of the drama, but she took advantage of the first number of the olio to display her capabilities as a dancer. Incidentally, she incited the ire of the Eagles by frequent references to the Hogan order, of which she claims to be a member. Sometimes her remarks amounted to invidious insinuation; and eventually the honored guests of the evening were provoked to retort. They directed cat calls and malamute howls at the winsome footlight fairy. Ordinarily such treatment would humiliate any member of the theatrical profession, for as a rule this class of people is most susceptible to applause or criticism. Gussie, however, when in a certain state of exhilaration, is evidently an exception to the rule which prevails among her associates. The taunts of the audience passed her by as the idle winds did Brutus some nineteen centuries ago. Indeed, this portion of the program was quite amusing to those disinterested persons who are neither Eagles nor Hogans.

Gussie, at that time, seems to have been in a perpetual state of exhilaration, because only ten days later the Stroller penned this social note, evidenced by another clipping:

The regular meeting of the Hogan order was held last Sunday evening and most of the meeting was devoted to a social session. All the Molly Hogans were attired in Easter costumes and their sixty-dollar bonnets and expensive silks added brilliance to the scene. Just before adjournment, Gussie Lamore created considerable excitement by falling into the punch bowl but she was quickly rescued.

The final clipping is also from *The Klondike Nugget*, with a date of June 25, 1902, and it was a reprint of an interview with Gussie that had appeared in the *Seattle Washingtonian*. The Stroller considered it valuable because it gives Gussie's own version of the famous egg story, which has already been mentioned in "The Eggs of

Dawson," and of which there must be a dozen different versions; maybe two dozen. The Stroller includes it here because it illuminates the lives of the famous sisters and because it is the last word he ever heard of them.

At the time of the interview, Gussie was playing at vaudeville houses in Spokane and vicinity. In describing her, the reporter said, "She is not a bad looking woman. She has genuine flaxen hair, a piquant expression, a pleasant smile, and is neat and stylish in appearance. She is still young but the dissipation incidental to the consumption of the champagne which the miners used to buy for her has left telltale marks on her pleasing countenance. Recently she unbosomed herself to this reporter as to the details of her marriage and her sisters' marriages to Swiftwater Bill Gates, as follows:

I met Swiftwater Bill in Dawson in the winter of '97. He certainly had the coin then. We were married after awhile. He lavished money on me, but I got dead sick of him. He had no sense and so I got to skating around with another guy. There was an egg famine came on in Dawson. Bill was interested in a store that got a consignment of 900 eggs which they were going to sell at a dollar apiece.

I'd already shaken Bill when I went down to the store to buy some eggs. Lordy, how I wanted some eggs for breakfast. Well, Bill was in the store when I gone in. He sees I want the eggs and while I'm talking with the clerk, see, he buys up the whole consignment at $1 apiece. Then he says to me, "Now, my dear, if you want eggs for breakfast, come home where you belong."

Well, hay, I was just dying for them eggs and I came to my milk like a lady. I gone home with Bill.

After that we lives in Dawson for awhile and then I comes out to the states with him. We stopped at Seattle and from there we went to 'Frisco.

In 'Frisco I introduced Bill to my family. Well, say, would you believe it, my sister Grace cops him out, steals him from me cold. I gets a divorce with a few alimonies and has her as the corespondent. The family is nothing if not on the square and after I gets the divorce Grace marries him.

Well, say, she lives with him a couple of weeks and quits him. She couldn't stand him at all. She leaves their room in the Baldwin and takes a flat. Bill he goes to her room while she's away, wraps her silverware and other valuables up in a sheet and carries them downtown on his back.

Finally Grace gets a divorce and her maiden name and then he steps in and takes up with my sister Nell. Nell only lived with him a week. She says she has a divorce from him, but I don't believe it. But it's a long time since they were together.

I didn't hear much of Bill until about a year ago when I read in the paper that he'd run away from Tacoma with his niece. Wouldn't that kill you? They goes to 'Frisco and Bill, as usual, goes flat broke. Bill hunts up sister Grace, the one that got her maiden name back, and tells her a hard luck story. Grace was always kind of soft, and what do you think? Why, she gave that slob enough money to pay his hotel bill and get out of town on.

Since then I haven't heard much of Bill. I'll bet money he's broke. I wouldn't be his niece for no money. Since I quit him I've been working in the show shops again and I'd rather do that than be the wife of any old Klondike millionaire. My other sister — one I haven't mentioned yet — is married to a Klondiker and he took her to Europe last summer. She says he treats her fine but I'm scared o' the breed. Say, I almost forgot to tell you that Bill tried to cop out the fourth sister o' mine after Nellie shook him, but he couldn't touch her with a ten-foot pole. That's where she's wiser than the rest of us.

"Are you and your sisters on good terms?" Miss Lamore was asked.

"Why certainly," was the reply. "Why should we fall out? Not over that stiff, I hope. We simply kept him in the family. When he got tired of one of us, we simply passed him along to the next one. If we hadn't, some other fairy would have got him, and there was no reason why all that coin shouldn't be kept in the Lamore family as long as possible."

With that the Stroller puts the Misses Lamore back in that deep recess of his mind, with the hope that they will stay there.

130

STAMPEDERS

THE STAMPEDER is unknown to present day residents of the Northland unless they have lived here for a quarter of a century or longer, and in that case the stampeder is only a memory. At one time and in some camps, fully ninety percent of the population was made up of stampeders, and in that day stampedes provided a large part of the recreation and entertainment of the camp. It is doubtful today that twenty percent of the people in the North know what a stampede really means, and it is for those who wallow in that sort of ignorance that this is written.

First, it should be made clear that a stampeder was not a prospector and he was not a miner. The stampeder was ever and anon chasing off after something the prospector had already discovered, or that the stampeder thought he had discovered, but if the stampeder happened to find the discovery, as he sometimes did, he lost interest in it at once. Real dyed-in-the-bean-pot prospectors had little use for stampeders. The latter tended to clutter up the trails, scatter or destroy the claim location stakes, disturb the pristine quiet of the creeks, and generally make nuisances of themselves. Some prospectors ignored the stampeders as much as they possibly could; others baited them and set traps for them, and sometimes they were able to do this at a modest but enjoyable profit to themselves.

Because of this difference in the temperament of the prospectors, there were two kinds of stampedes—those that were "set" and those that were self-starters and just happened. In their end result they were identical, but the beginnings were somewhat different and the Stroller will explain them both, starting with those that were "set" by a prospector.

A long-haired prospector comes into camp, looking worn, bedraggled and mysterious. He does not necessarily have to be bedraggled but he must look mysterious, and any prospector who cannot look mysterious when the occasion requires has not learned the rudiment of his trade. Someone remembers that the prospector left camp three months before, heading for the headwaters of some distant creek and carrying a pick and gold pan, a slab of bacon, some beans and a few pounds of flour. Now he has returned for more grub but he would not have returned so soon if he had not eaten up the flour so he could use the sack to patch his pants. The prospector is uncommunicative as well as mysterious as he reaches camp, but after a while someone edges up to him and casually asks whether he found anything worth staking.

The prospector looks wise and diffident for a short time, but finally he delves into the interior of his frayed and frazzled raiment and brings to light a chunk of gold quartz which probably originated in Leadville, Colorado. The quartz is liberally studded with gold and soon more men have gathered around to examine it and discuss it. But when the owner is asked where he got it, he shuts up like a clam, snatches back the sample, drops it into its hiding place, and stomps off.

The prospector has a glorious time for a few days and shows his sample many times. Also, he is invited to drink many times, and he drinks many times. His wonderful find soon becomes the talk of the camp and is discussed in bars, barbershops and bunkhouses. But the location of the find is not yet revealed. The time is not ripe, although it is ripening fast as the supply of free drinks begins to dwindle.

Then the promoter appears on the scene. Usually he is a bartender and he whispers to a few select customers that if ten men will chip in fifty dollars each, the prospector will put them wise to the exact location of his discovery. No, the prospector can't go with them himself as he has promised the fellow he left on the ground that he will not reveal its location. But he will draw a map and give directions that will enable them to find the place without any trouble.

The fifties are unobtrusively slipped to the bartender and during the silent watches of the following night ten or a dozen dog taams depart from the camp, quietly and without the emphatic utterances usual to dog drivers. The stampeders are off to seek their fortunes on a distant and sometimes mythical creek.

In the meantime, and before the stampeders can return, the prospector has collected his percentage of the take from the bartender, got another outfit together and headed out in some other direction. He has had his fun, completed his drunk and acquired another grubstake in the process.

The stampeders return a few days later with their hearts full of venom and their shoes full of blisters, cussing the prospector as a monumental liar and cussing themselves for having been taken in. But the prospector is not there to hear them, and when he returns a few months later the chances are good that he will be able to work the same trick again, using the same mysterious air and the same old chunk of Leadville quartz. If the same old suckers are not ready for hooking, another bunch will take their place for the population is constantly changing.

In the self-starting stampede, on the other hand, the prospector involved does everything he can to avoid setting it off. He has probably discovered good colors in a previously untouched area and he wants to save it for himself and a few close friends. The last thing he wants is a stampede. So, when the time comes to replenish his bean sack, he takes a circuitous route, throws out several false trails, and sneaks into camp as unobtrusively as possible, wearing frayed clothes and an optimistic look. The latter is as natural to him as the former and only a few prospectors, after long practice, have learned to conceal their optimism. For a prospector must be an optimist and a man who is not an optimist does not become a prospector but stays with faro dealing, bartending, news reporting or some other trade for which his gloomy outlook fits him.

But the prospector's efforts toward obscurity are in vain. The stampeders have their ears to the ground and their eyes on any prospector who happens along, and one of them spots him and passes the word that it looks as though Old Beans and Bacon has found something. The second stampeder gives the news to a third, with the added information that the find made by Old Beans and Bacon is very rich, at least half an ounce to the pan. By the time the story reaches the fifth or sixth stampeder, the strike Old B and B has made is so rich that it is necessary to mix gravel with the gold in order to pan it. Thus the story makes the rounds. All liars are not necessarily stampeders, but all stampeders are liars, either natural-born or by training, and each firmly believes the lies of the other.

Someone remembers that Old Beans and Bacon was seen sinking a hole in such and such a location six months before, and another stampede is on. Fabulous prices are paid for dog teams and a stampeder who is short of funds may charter a team on a 50-50 basis. Then, in the dead of night, when all others who are not busy dancing or gambling are asleep, from a dozen to fifty men slip away in the darkness, confident that within a day or two they will be rich. And a week or so later they drag back with void and empty interior realms and frost-bitten ears and noses, swearing that they had panned a dozen holes put down by Old B and B without finding a single color. And this is probably the truth, for if Old B and B has been ingenious in covering his tracks, they never got within miles of his strike.

In the early days of the North, every community had a flock of those chronic stampeders who would take the trail on a moment's notice and travel a hundred miles without rest. And now and then they would find something worthwhile, stake some claims and hurry back to the recorder's office to record the locations. But that was always the end of it. They never paid any further attention to the locations. They were stampeders, not miners.

The Stroller has known many stampedes and hundreds of stampeders and he has been "stamped" a few times himself, sometimes taking the trail and sometimes sending a proxy. If he went himself, it was in the firm belief that he would return a millionaire. And if he sent a substitute to locate a claim for him, the Stroller would busily cultivate the characteristics of a millionaire until the party returned. At such times he would become unusually generous, no matter whether it was boosting Zion or boosting the pot where a few were sitting in.

There have been many strange and unusual stampedes in the North and the Stroller remembers one that took place a few years ago and of which he was the innocent cause. Two men were panning on a placer bar at the forks of McCormick's Creek when they came across a trace of nicotine. Thinking that it came from a ledge of tobacco, they followed the trace up the left fork for seven miles and came upon a corncob pipe the Stroller had lost while hunting moose three years before. Having been fooled themselves, they decided to fool others and started a rumor that they had located a veritable mountain of hard-pressed Navy plug. One of the greater stampedes in the history of the North followed.

Today, prospectors are so scarce as to be curiosities, while the chronic stampeder has wholly vanished. All that remains are the stories of early stampedes, all of which are warranted to be true. But never has the Stroller seen the stampeder so accurately and fittingly described as in the following, written by Mr. H. Beeman, former secretary of the Mining Bureau, Vancouver Board of Trade:

> The traveler knocked at the gates that blocked
>   The way to the heavenly home,
> And Saint Peter came and asked his name
>   And whither he had lately come.
> He didn't expect that he'd be checked
>   For he'd ever been a ready host,
> And he'd drop his pack at any man's shack,
>   From the Rockies to the coast.
> But if 'twas Peter's whim, 'twas all right with him,
>   He'd put up with the slight delay,
> And he felt no shame to give his name
>   And whence he had made his way.
> Now down below, it was just plain "Joe,"
>   The label they'd tagged him with,
> And it did him proud to be one of the crowd
>   Who had borne the name of Smith.
>
> And as to the place, he'd say to his face,
>   Saint Peter had nothing to show
> Like the mirrored sight of the peaks snow-white,
>   In the calm of the lakes below;
> Or the daylight's shrink from red to pink,
>   To yellow, to inky pall,
> From the rocky ledge to the water's edge,
>   As the evening shadows fall.

Saint Peter, though mild, got Joe quite riled,
When he asked where such sights might be.
Sure, everyone knew—just as I or you—
Where else but in old B.C.
Then the Saint was told how he'd searched for gold—
Death had dashed from his lips the cup—
But Saint Peter said, as he shook his head,
That that section was quite full up.

Said the Saint: "It's clear they would make for here,
When they hit the last, long trail,
For they've all been told that the streets are gold,
But the sight of it soon gets stale;
There's no 'might be found'—it's all proven ground,
And they find it a trifle slow.
The moss-backs ache for a good grubstake,
When the spring is melting the snow."

Though the gates clanged to, Joe wasn't through,
He was bound to get inside,
So he sat to think, on the Great Void brink,
How to make them open wide.
He thought for awhile and then a smile—
Like sunshine after the rain—
Spread over his face, and he took his place
At the gates, and knocked again.

The Saint appeared and, nothing afeared,
Joe said he would like to send
To Jack McAdoo, of Cariboo,
A message straight from a friend.
"Make no mistake, it's 'Jitney Jake',
He's the only one you'll tell;
And drawing him near, hissed in his ear,
"There's a placer strike down in Hell!"

With a glow of content, then back he went
To his seat on the Outer Rim,
They were all alike, and he knew he'd hike,
If such a message had come to him.
And soon they sped, with a stealthy tread,
Some he thought he never would see;
They were of every date, from fifty-eight
To nineteen and twenty-three.

At last to the door came Peter once more,
And he said there was room to spare,
But naught heeded Joe, as he muttered low:
"Gosh! Maybe there's something there!"
So with eyes ablaze in an eager gaze,
And the look of a man possessed,
He hoisted his pack on his old bent back,
And hurried off after the rest!

NIGGER
JIM DAUGHERTY

"PROMENADE to the bar!"

That was a frequent and welcome cry in Nigger Jim's New Pavilion at Dawson around the turn of the century when gold was flowing from nearly every creek in the Klondike country and the whole Northland was in bloom.

And "promenade to the bar" is what Nigger Jim Daugherty did at Fairbanks last week, on September 21, (1924). But it was a different bar than he had ever stood before on earth.

James Daugherty was one of those referred to in those early Dawson days as a "real sourdough." By this was meant that he had arrived in the North before the Gold Rush of 1897 and 1898 attracted the Sam Brothers—Flot and Jet—and the thousands of their kin. He was a member of the relatively small band that did the real pioneering in the gold country, a hardy and self-reliant lot who seldom needed or called for help. But when one of those men did require assistance, through some misfortune or other, his fellow pioneers were ever ready to lend a helping hand, a quality that was lacking in many of those who came later.

James Daugherty came north at least as early as 1895 and perhaps a little earlier and he went first to the Fortymile country, where the first real strike of the Interior had been made several years before. Later on he moved to the Birch Creek diggings and made his headquarters at the famed log cabin town of Circle City on the Yukon, where he was a member of the Circle City Miners Association. It was at Circle City late in the year 1896 that James Daugherty acquired his nickname, Nigger Jim.

To help pass the time during the long winter months, the members of the Miners Association decided to put on a minstrel show, and Casey Moran was placed in charge of getting it up and directing it. Scouting through the camp for talent for the show, Casey made an early choice of Jim, who had been born in Alabama during the Civil War and could handle Negro dialect to perfection. In addition, Jim had a considerable store of "Darkey" songs. He was a big, handsome man with a fair voice, and when he blacked up and sang his songs and cracked his jokes in that dialect from the deep South, he was the hit of the show. The show was voted a complete success and Casey Moran was awarded a gold ring as a token of appreciation for his efforts while James Daugherty got a nickname that clung to him.

When gold was discovered in the Klondike the following year, Nigger Jim headed for the scene and opened one of the first saloons in the new camp of Dawson. He called it The Pavilion and hired a man to run it for him while he prospected the creeks and rushed from thither to thence with the others who were early on the ground. Jim staked some good claims but he did not work them himself. Instead, he went to England the following spring and sold his holdings for a good price.

It was late in the year when Jim got back to Dawson, and by that time the big fire of October 14, 1898, had swept away The Pavilion Saloon along with most of the other business buildings in town. Jim put his newly acquired capital to work and with it he built a combined saloon, gambling house, dance hall and theater, all under one roof, and proudly named it Nigger Jim's New Pavilion.

That same year, 1899, Jim married Lottie Oatley, one of a team of buck and wing dancers and singers known as the Oatley Sisters, although one of the "sisters" was actually the mother, who also conducted a dancehall.

For two years after he opened the New Pavilion, Nigger Jim could neither spend nor give away the money as fast as it came his way, although he did the best he could along both lines. He was a genial man and he liked to stand at the end of the bar and greet his friends. Everyone was Jim's friend in those days, especially the people who wanted something from him. These were legion. Jim was always good for a grubstake, although he was probably well aware that few of those he grubstaked were going to find anything worth finding and that most of them weren't even going to look. There was always a big free lunch at the end of Jim's bar, and it wasn't just crackers and cheese, either. Everybody was welcome to it, and there were men who lived in Dawson for a whole year without ever eating except off the end of Nigger Jim's bar. The money kept rolling in and Jim kept handing it out, but even so he was reckoned a rich man by 1901.

Then the wind changed. By the middle of 1902 Jim was down and out, flat broke and flat on his back, too. He had been stricken with partial paralysis and for twenty months he was unable to walk and he had to be lifted from his bed to a chair and then back to the bed again. This was quite a task, as Jim had also partaken unstintingly of the appetizing dishes on the end of the bar and he weighed fully three hundred pounds when he was stricken. Those were dark days for Jim and Lottie and their little daughter, who had also been named Lottie. The drifter crowd in Dawson, the ones who had hung around the New Pavilion with their hands out for so long, quickly forgot him. But the old-timers, the ones Jim had known in pre-Gold Rush days, stayed by him and did what they could to help.

After Jim lost about half his former weight and could be handled more easily, his friends would frequently send a transfer wagon and a couple of men to bring him down town and drive him around from place to place to make afternoon calls. Jim began to improve then, and by the summer of 1904 he could walk again. It was then that Lottie, having gotten Jim back on his feet, took their little girl and went to Fairbanks where she entered vaudeville. Jim remained in Dawson where his friends cared for him as he continued to improve. But none of the vast sums of money he had given away in the palmy days ever came his way again.

In 1906 Nigger Jim also went to Fairbanks, but by then Lottie had obtained a divorce. Later that year she joined the Australians, a company of barnstormers who had played their way to the Interior, making enough at each one night stand to take them on to the next. And when they "stood" out of Fairbanks, Lottie was with them, although by that time little remained of the lustre that had surrounded the Oatley Sisters seven years earlier, and what little was left was very dim.

A few years later Nigger Jim also left the country and went to Washington State, where he is reported to have worked around the logging camps, although in what capacity, the Stroller does not know. Then, when the new camp of Anchorage reached the budding stage with the building of the government railroad, Jim returned north. He was around Knik for a time, serving as a night watchman and doing other light work, and he was last employed by the Alaska Railroad in the vicinity of Healy. He was still genial, still a friend of everyone, and there was never a moan about his hard luck. It was while he was at Healy that he was again stricken, this time with what was thought to be appendicitis. He was taken to the hospital in Fairbanks and Dr. Romig, the railroad doctor, examined him and found that the trouble was more deeply seated and was incurable.

James Daugherty died in the hospital in Fairbanks, and he died poor if not entirely broke. Had he possessed even a small part of what he gave away and loaned out, and of what the bartenders and hangers-on around the New Pavilion stole from him, he would have died surrounded by luxury with medical specialists and high-priced nurses. But it is unlikely that he would have had any more real friends than he did as just Poor Old Nigger Jim, and in all probability he would not have been one bit happier.

ICE
POOLS

GAY AND GLADSOME springtime is again fast approaching, the season of the year when, during those halcyon days during which the Northland was in full flower, fresh eggs, fresh meat, and fresh cheechako dancehall girls were all imported to Dawson over the ice and the town rejoiced and was exceedingly thankful in consequence. For, during the dark and dreary months of the long winter the eggs in Dawson had grown ripe, the meat had acquired a flavor the Englishmen described as "high," and the dancehall girls who had been on the job since the previous season were becoming stale and passé.

And this was also the season of the year when the ice pool flourished throughout the North, as it still does. But where today the ice pools have been consolidated into one big pool for each community, in earlier years they were almost universally conducted by the saloons and the number of pools in any town depended on the number of saloons the town could afford. (Perhaps "afford" is not the proper word, as many towns had more saloons than the cash books of the wholesale dealers indicated they could support.)

A ticket on an ice pool, in those early years, was usually a secondary consideration. The prime object in approaching the bar was a drink. Once that had been purchased and consumed, if there was any dust left in the poke and if the bartender suggested it, the customer was likely to take a chance that he could correctly guess the day, hour and minute the river ice would begin to move in its annual break-up. Each guess cost a dollar and the only limit on the number of guesses registered by any one individual was his own cash reserve. The customer received a ticket for each guess, with the date and time of his guess inscribed upon it. The same information, along with his name, was recorded by the knight of the white apron in a book kept for that purpose.

The "house" got no commission for selling the tickets, but when the ice went out and the lucky guesser, with a few dozen of his friends tagging along, came in to collect his winnings, the "house" got what was coming to it. And that, in the parlance of the day, was plenty. The winner modestly accepted the congratulations of his friends upon his good fortune, and the friends modestly accepted the drinks the winner bought them. It was a modest performance all the way around. Also, if the lucky guesser wished to try his luck further with a play on a card in the faro layout or on the little ball that traversed the rim of the roulette wheel, those accommodations were available and handy. The total result was that ice pool winnings, as a rule, did not get very far from the paint and pool emporiums where they were won.

The memory of the Stroller wanders back to the spring of the year 1901 when the ice on the mighty Yukon, after having been moored solidly for almost seven months, began to move majestically northward in front of the then busy city of Dawson. It was a Sunday evening and a vast crowd thronged the Auditorium Theatre, the occasion being the production of a sacred concert. The reason it was a sacred concert was that the Lord's Day Act of the Dominion of Canada clearly stipulated that shows could be staged on Sunday only if they were "sacred." The show had to be billed as "sacred" whether there was anything sacred about it or not. Usually there was a hymn of some kind on the program to satisfy the law, while such Irish comedians as John Sullivan, Ed Dolan and Tom Rooney, and a number of other celebrated performers, male and female, filled out the bill to satisfy the patrons, the law being more easily satisfied than the patrons, many of whom could be classed as wild and unfettered.

On this particular Sunday evening, the orchestra had just finished the opening number—something classic in Saul or somebody else—and the curtain was trembling on the rise when the whistle on the Northern Commercial Company power house cut loose a blast that rattled the windows for a dozen blocks around. It was the signal that the ice was moving.

The Stroller once saw a show house in the deep South suddenly emptied when two gentlemen who held stubs for the same reserved seat decided to draw guns rather than straws for the honor, but he never saw any place more quickly emptied than was the Auditorium Theatre when the ice moved at 8:15 p.m. on May 8, 1901. Most of those present held one or more tickets in several ice pools, and while it was not necessary to see the ice move in order to win, there was a certain satisfaction in watching it. The moving ice meant that the long winter was finally ended and that the steamboats would soon be running again, and consequently there was a mighty gathering at the river that Sunday evening, the bank of the river being but a block and a half from the Auditorium Theatre.

It was almost an hour later that the concert was resumed, and as no return checks had been issued, the crowd that moved from the river to the theater was enough to fill two theaters. It was a case of first come, first seated, and arguments settled in the alley in the rear. The program was very well received that night. Mike Hooley never sang "All Bound 'Round With a Woolen String" with more gusto and vim; Chris Moran rendered "A Cross-

146

Eyed Bear" very effectively, and there was great interest in High-Kicking Hattie's specialty number which consisted of—well, perhaps the Stroller had better state what it did not consist of, and that was anything "sacred."

Because the ice had started to move on a Sunday, when the front doors of all the paint stores were locked and the Town Patrol of the Royal Northwest Mounted Police became suspicious if more than two people were seen heading for a back door at one time, the winners of the various ice pools were permitted to wait until the following day to collect their winnings. And by the next day, the excitement having died down, the strings of followers were not nearly so long as they would have been if it had gone out on a week day. It was said, in fact, that one winner of $550 still had $75 in his pocket when he returned to his claim on King Solomon Hill late Monday afternoon. He had eaten a hearty breakfast and a good lunch and left Dawson early in the afternoon, before the dancehall janes were astir. Otherwise it is doubtful that he would have reached the claim before sometime Tuesday, and then only after having breakfasted off cheese and crackers at the end of a bar. The owners of the saloons and gambling houses were not entirely happy with the way things turned out that year. They considered it bad for business and there was talk of getting up a By-Law or an Order in Council to prevent the ice moving on a Sunday, but nothing came of it.

The ice has formed on the Yukon and the Tanana many times since that year 1901, only to break away in the gay and glorious springtime and start its journey toward Bering Sea. And in the years that have come and gone, ice pools have been commercialized and a spirit of greed has succeeded the spirit of gambling that once characterized them. Chances are taken in the ice pools today with a view to acquiring wealth, while in former days the venture was prompted more by the fun of gambling in a mild way than by anything else. If you won, in those days, it was all right. And if some other fellow won, that was all right, too, and he would invite everybody within range to name his pizen. And in those gaudy days, now long gone, the pizen was worth naming.

IRON
SHOD

DESPITE ALL OF Dawson's gayety and glitter during the years the Stroller lived there and for many years afterward, the town's principal purpose and reason for existing was the sober one of acting as a supply center for the rich Klondike gold mining region which fanned out along the multitude of creeks and over the hills behind the town. An enormous tonnage of cargo, consisting of goods of every imaginable variety, was delivered at the Dawson waterfront every summer by the steamboats and barges which came upriver from the Yukon's mouth and the steamboats and scows which came downriver from the head of navigation. And while much of the cargo was consumed in Dawson, a great deal of it had to be delivered to the mines, some of which were forty and fifty miles from town. This delivery was handled, in the early days, by the freighters who used wagons and pack trains during the months of summer and sleds after snow covered the ground.

One of the largest of the freighting outfits was the Bartlett Brothers, consisting of Mike, Al and Ed Bartlett. They owned many wagons and teams and pack horses and in addition they shipped a hundred pack mules to Dawson in 1898. The mules were used mainly for packing to the more distant creeks where the trails were poorest and the route likely to be treacherous, the brothers claiming that mules were superior to horses on such routes. Each mule carried a pack of around two hundred pounds and as the charges for packing to the more distant creeks ran as high as seventy-five cents a pound, each mule was capable of earning for its owners something like $150 every four days, which was the usual time required for a round trip. Mostly they returned to town light as there was little freight to be moved from the mines to Dawson, but even so the operation was quite profitable. Of course, the pack animals did not earn anything at all during the winter months, but there was little expense to keeping them during this period as most of them were turned loose to forage for themselves. There was grass in most of the valleys and plenty of willows along the creeks and some of them, especially the mules, hung around the mining camps and were fed potato peelings and left-over pancakes and other tidbits. There was work for some of them until late in the fall, after the busy season was ended, when they were rented out to the market hunters who killed moose, caribou and sometimes mountain sheep for sale in town, and sometimes to private hunters who were going after their own meat supply. It was not at all uncommon in Dawson about the time of the freeze-up to see a long pack train laden with quarters of fresh-killed meat.

One year about the middle of October three Englishmen who had newly arrived in the country and had observed these meat-laden pack trains decided that there must be a good deal of sport connected with moose hunting and that they would give it a try. They sought advice on how to go about this and their seeking took them to the places where advice on all subjects was freely and bountifully available, and this of course was in the saloons. And since most of the people they consulted were Canadians or Americans who had small use for Englishmen who had just arrived from the old country and were still addicted to the use of the long glawse, they were handed a great

150

many packages of advice, most of which was conflicting and little of which was sound. They were advised to take a pack animal or two to carry back the product of their chase, but as a matter of economy they decided to get the moose first and then to worry about getting it out.

The three Englishmen hiked up the Klondike River with their guns and camping equipment and spent a week beating around in the brush. None of them had ever seen a moose except after it had been drawn and quartered and they had no experience at hunting or anything else connected with the outdoors. As they did not know where to look for moose, they did not find any and when the week ended they gave up in disgust and headed back to Dawson. Night overtook them when they were about four miles from town and they decided to make a final camp and finish the journey in the morning.

They rolled out of their blankets at dawn the next day and while two members of the party were cooking breakfast the third took a gun and wandered off into the brush. A few minutes later a shot was heard, followed by excited yells: "I say, you chaps, come quick as you can. I've just killed us a splendid cow moose."

The others became as excited as he and rushed to the scene, leaving their last mess of bacon to burn in the pan. They surveyed the kill and exclaimed over it and their first thought was to hurry to town where they could brag about their skill and good fortune and secure the services of a pack animal to fetch in the quarry. There was some discussion about leaving one member of the party to guard the kill, but none wanted to miss the thrill of being in on the first telling of the tale and it was decided that the meat would be safe until they returned. They hurriedly hacked off some hunks of the animal to prove that they had actually killed something and rushed pell mell down the trail for Dawson. There they made the rounds of the

151

saloons to relate the exciting events of the hunt and display the proof of their prowess. The celebration had reached its third round and the glawses were being filled for a fourth when one of the Englishmen grew thoughtful.

"I say, you chaps," he said. "There is something about a moose I didn't know before, or else this bally critter was very unusual, don't cha know? But this moose had been shod; it has iron shoes on all four feet. Extraordinary, what?"

NORTHLAND
MEMORIES

HUNDREDS OF EVENTS, large and small, have been recorded on the scroll of time during the years the Stroller has been observing undone and sodden humanity in the Northland, and now and again one of those events floats to the surface of the Stroller's memory.

There was the time the Stroller entered a Second Avenue grocery store in Dawson to buy a loaf of rye bread and a chunk of bologna and was almost run over by a bold-faced young woman who rushed out the door carrying half of an onion in her hand.

"What was that about," the Stroller asked.

"I don't know," said the grocer. "She rushed in here and demanded half an onion; said she'd be back to pay for it and tell me how she used it."

Ever curious, the Stroller borrowed a knife and fixed himself a sandwich and before long the young woman returned, her eyes red but with a broad smile on her face.

"Did you see an old duffer headed toward the dock an hour ago with an old valise in his hand?" she asked.

The grocer answered in the affirmative and she continued: "Well, the old chap has been soft on me for some time past and I have been working him for all I could get. He left today on a hurried visit to his family outside, and as he will be back on one of the last steamers, I want to stay solid with him. So, I wrapped that half onion in my handkerchief and went down to the boat to see him off. Every time I would put the handkerchief to my eyes the tears would come and the old fool actually thought I was crying because he was leaving me. He gave me a hundred dollars and said, 'Don't cry, little girl; I'll be back soon.' Some of the girls around Dawson may be better looking than me, but when it comes to leg pulling, I don't take a back seat for any of them."

She paid for the onion, let out a harsh laugh, and went out the door. The grocer said, "Well, I'll be gol-darned."

* * *

The Stroller, after asking the bartender to put a squirt of lemon in it, was deep in conversation with two of his friends. One was a lawyer who was often called Necessity (he knew no law); the other was the Shirtless Kid, a former booster who had improved his station in life and was now selling a mixture of brick dust and flour to warehouse owners for rat poison.

Our conversation was interrupted by a voice that said, "Up against the real thing? Well, I rather guess I am!"

The speaker was a well-dressed, robust young man who looked to be a stranger to all kinds of manual labor. He continued, without being invited to do so:

"Me and her came here last summer and she has ever since been able to give me on an average $10 every day, to say nothing of an occasional $20 and sometimes $50; and as she has also paid the grocery and laundry bills, I have managed to get along very comfortably here, although I have only worked eight shifts since I struck the town.

"It is an old saying that trouble never comes singly and in our case it is verified. Only Wednesday night I went down town, got to playing bank and dropped every cent of cash me and her had and left tabs for $250 more. Within the next 24 hours an order from the police put her out of business and I am left to starve. She has been

154

bawling up at the cabin all day and says she will take in washing before I shall do any kind of work that will spoil my hands for dealing. But if she is going to do anything she will have to get a move on mighty quick or I'll shake her; I don't tie up to no girl that can't support me. There's lots of us fellows who have the bread taken from our mouths by this order which makes the girls quit box rustlin' If they can't hustle the miners in the boxes, why do they have boxes in the dance halls? If it wasn't that the police would likely throw the whole push of us in jail and put us to sawin' wood, about 40 of us fellows who are vitally interested because of having our beasts of burden put out of business, would march up there in a body and ask to have the girls allowed to go back to work and keep us 'till we can get out on the boats next spring."

With a sigh that started in his patent leather boots, the man whose support had been legislated away sauntered over to the faro table. The Stroller turned to resume his conversation with his friends, but they were gone. Departed.

Obviously they didn't care for the company. The Stroller agreed and forthwith left the premises.

* * *

In Dawson, the Stroller frequently visited the police court in search of news. In one case he remembers it was charged that a dog had stolen a whole ham from a cache twelve feet high. The owner of the dog, who operated a restaurant in town, claimed that it was not possible for his dog to have climbed into the cache, but the owner of the ham swore that the dog, in 50-below weather, blew its breath on one of the posts of the cache, forming steps by which it climbed up and grabbed the ham.

Moreover, said the erstwhile owner of the ham, although the dog chewed all the meat off the bone, he believed that ham bone was still in the possession of the restaurant owner. He asked to be permitted to subpoena it as evidence. The magistrate took that under advisement. The Stroller knew, however, that the statement was true; he had eaten soup made from the identical ham bone dozens of times.

* * *

The Stroller was living in Whitehorse and editing a newspaper called the *Whitehorse Star* during one especially heated political campaign. While the Stroller attempts to maintain a calm and judicious attitude at such times, in that one he got carried away and said things about George Black, a Dawson candidate, that he perhaps could not prove in court. Black was defeated and he demanded a public retraction and an apology for what he called "Libelous and Criminal assertions," else he would institute such proceedings as the law provides in such cases.

The Stroller decided to apologize, and as what is worth doing is worth doing well, this is what he wrote:

> To George Black, Esq., Dawson,
> Dear Sir: Not being a lawyer and, therefore, not able to conduct his own case in court, the editor of the *Star* hereby tenders to you his apology and retraction of the offensive 'Libelous and Criminal' assertions published in said newspaper on the 15th of January. Owing to the fact that the ground is covered with snow as with a mantle, biblically speaking, you will please excuse the formality of the editor rubbing his nose in the dust and will take the statement of a willingness to do so, were conditions favorable, for the deed.

The statements you characterize 'absolutely false and without foundation' were wired to the *Star* from Dawson in a telegraph signed 'News' and you will accommodate the editor of the *Star* if you will call at that scissors and paste emporium and lick the *Star* correspondent. To insure getting the right man you had better take a punch at the whole bunch. (If this can be construed as an attempt to incite a riot, he apologizes for it, too.)

Anyhow, the editor of the *Star* apologizes, retracts and hereby requests his readers to expunge, wipe out from their blackboards or their think tanks, the 'Libelous and Criminal' statements contained in an issue of said newspaper of the 15th of January. Angels could do no more!

Repentently but lovingly yours,
E. J. White,
Editor *Weekly Star*
Subscriptions $5 per year in advance.

* * *

FRANK
SLAVIN

A GREAT DEAL of water, some of it carrying pay but much of it moving only barren sand and gravel, rolled down the sluice boxes between the first and last times the Stroller heard of Frank Slavin. The Stroller was a callow youth in Florida when Slavin, who was known as the Sydney Cornstalk, fought his way out of his native Australia, met all challenges of South Africa and England and was crowned the heavyweight champion of the Empire. And after John L. Sullivan, having drawn the color line and refusing to fight Negro Peter Jackson, also side-stepped a match with Slavin, there were many who felt that the latter should have been awarded the world championship by default. But Sullivan wanted nothing to do with Slavin, for the latter had required only three rounds to knock out Jack Burke, the tough Irishman who had stayed five rounds with the great John L. And when Jim Corbett, having wrested the crown from Sullivan, also avoided a bout with Slavin, the latter became very bitter. All of this the Stroller followed from a distance and little did he then dream that he would one day hire the great Australian to pile wood at fifty cents a cord.

It was in the fall of 1897 that Frank Slavin, after having barnstormed over much of the United States and Canada putting on exhibition bouts, first came north to Dawson. He was in company with Joseph Whiteside Boyle who had been his sparring partner and who was to become famed as Klondike Boyle and then, during the Great War, as Colonel Boyle. But Frank remained in Dawson only a short while on that occasion and it was in May or early June of 1898 that the Stroller first met him in Skagway. Frank was on his way back to Dawson and with him was the previously mentioned Peter Jackson whom many considered the greatest fighter of them all.

Neither man was flush with money and they decided to stage a ten-round bout there in Skagway. Both men were past the heydey of their fighting careers but they could still give good accounts of themselves in the ring. They had met twice before in serious combat. The first time was a barroom roughhouse in Australia, with no decision. The second time was a ring classic in London, with the Prince of Wales in the audience, and Frank was knocked out by the Negro. In Skagway it was announced that the winner would take the gate receipts and a $10,000 side bet. Of course, neither man had $10,000 or anything like it, but that was thrown in to stimulate interest, and it did.

The biggest hall in Skagway was packed to the rafters an hour before the fight, which was to start at 9 o'clock. But when that time came, there was no sign of the gladiators, and by 10 o'clock the crowd was getting boisterous and unruly. At 10:30 the fans filed out and received refunds at the door. The fight was called off because Peter Jackson, who was even then in the last stages of tuberculosis, had poured too freely of the fluid extract of rye, the only remedy for his incessant cough, and was in no condition to appear. Peter Jackson turned back from Skagway, but Frank Slavin went on to Dawson where he was a ring favorite and the idol of the fistic fans for several years.

He was a colorful character, both in appearance and speech. Standing six foot one and a half inches, his light complexion and long, windmilling arms had won him the nickname Sydney Cornstalk, although for some of his fights he was billed as the Sydney Slasher. Frank retained every trace of his original Australian accent and pronunciation, and in England he had picked up and added to them a variety of Whitechapel expressions and Cockney epithets, none of which could be classified as delicate. As for fighting, he was willing to take on anyone at any time, in or out of the ring. It was the late Sam Dunham who, on his return to New York in the fall of 1898, wrote a poem entitled "Since I Came Back From Dawson," one verse of which read:

> I have just returned from Dawson
> Where I saw Frank Slavin spar,
> And saw his late antagonists
> Reviving at the bar,
> While Frank shook hands with all his friends
> And loudly did declare,
> That he could lick Fitzsimmons, too,
> If Fitz were only there.

Between 1898 and 1904 many pugilists and would-be pugilists showed up in Dawson and attempted to wrest the Yukon championship from the veteran Australian, but until the latter year none was able to do so, although Frank took severe punishment on several occasions. One of the many who tried was a young giant who reached Dawson late in the year 1901 and introduced himself as Frank Kennedy. He was a wrestler and came north with the announced intention of picking up some easy money, which was the same thing that brought a majority of Dawson residents to the country. But after he had defeated the best the camp had to offer, including the former world champion, Colonel McLaughlin, and Ole March, the pride of the Scandinavians, first singly and then together, taking them on alternately with but two minutes of rest between rounds, Kennedy ran out of opponents and decided to try his hand at pugilism. He issued a challenge to Slavin and it was of course accepted.

Never had such a crowd turned out to witness a prize fight in Dawson. Men swarmed in from distant creeks by dog sled and stage, and many who risked their dust on Kennedy made their breakfasts on cheese and crackers at the end of Tom Chisholm's bar and returned to the distant creeks afoot. Having had little or no experience with the fists, Kennedy took a beating from Slavin for four rounds. Then, in the fifth round, he made a rush for the old-timer, wrapped him in a wrestling hold and deliberately fell forward on top of him. The fight was awarded to Slavin on the foul and Kennedy took the next stage for Whitehorse and the Outside. It soon became known that the man who called himself Kennedy was none other than Frank Gotch, the wrestling champion, and some who claimed to be in the know said the foul had been prearranged and that they split the purse fifty-fifty. Maybe they did; the Stroller does not know.

But all this time, Frank Slavin was traveling the trail that leads to the Sunset Shore. Age was creeping up on him and before long it was moving faster than a creep. The Stroller had a ringside seat the night Frank's prize fighting career ended. A much younger and faster man had showed up and Frank, still confident, had accepted his challenge to a ten round bout. Canadian law would not permit a finish fight and pugilistic events were billed as Sparring Exhibitions, but for the old warhorse it was a fight to the finish, and for him that night was the finish. It was in the seventh round that he staggered to the ropes, ejected a mouthful of water mixed with teeth, held up his hand for silence, and announced: "It ain't no use to continue the bloody go."

Poor old Frank was defeated, but he wasn't whipped. He realized, however, that his fighting days were over and never again did he appear in a prize ring. He worked as bouncer at the Monte Carlo for a time, and his old sparring partner, Joe Boyle, who was by then a millionaire or close to it, helped him out and found odd jobs for him.

In those years, the Stroller customarily bought twenty cords of wood each fall and the wood had to be carried in from the street and piled in the woodshed. It was some years after "the bloody go" and when the first load of ten cords was dumped, the Missouri Kid, Tip Top Daisy's man, carried it in and piled it all in about six hours and received his five dollars. When the second load was delivered Frank Slavin solicited the job at the going rate of fifty cents a cord and was awarded the contract. It took him the best part of four days to do the job and for a time the Stroller was fearful that he would not make it.

The last time the Stroller saw Frank Slavin he was heading for the Outside and stopped at Whitehorse, where he accepted an invitation to breakfast. Out of regard for his stomach, which he said had been bothering him, he turned down ham and eggs in favor of prunes, toast, jam and coffee. Not long after that the Great War came on and Frank, at the age of 62, showed the stuff he was made of by volunteering to fight for Britain. He was turned down at first, but when the Germans were unchecked in 1915, he was accepted and went to France but had to be invalided home before long.

In opening this article, the Stroller mentioned the first time he heard of Frank Slavin. He will close it by telling of the last time he heard of him. This was on Monday of the present week when a press dispatch told of the burial of the winner of scores of battles, at Vancouver, B.C., on Saturday, October 19, 1929. But the press dispatch was wrong in one particular. It gave Frank's age as 64. He was actually 77.

162

THE
HOT CAKE
KID

A RECENT MAIL brought the Stroller a letter from far off Australia. It was signed by one J. H. P. Smythe who was inquiring about his brother, Henry William Otis Smythe. The latter, according to his brother, was a baker by trade, had started for the Klondike early in 1898, and had written home but once since then. The name Smythe failed to stir up so much as a tinkle under the Stroller's bonnet and he was about to drop the letter into the wastebasket when a postscript caught his eye:

"My brother said in his letter that he was sometimes known around Skagway as the Hot Cake Kid."

The Stroller's memory picked up with that and began to hit on all of its cylinders as it spun back over the years. The Hot Cake Kid! Of course he knew the Hot Cake Kid, and so did a lot of others in the North, many of them to their sorrow. He was one of hundreds of Australians who landed in Skagway in the year 1898 enroute to the Klondike. And the Australians were reckoned "easy pickins" by Captain Jefferson Randolph Smith and his crowd, who were picking everything pickable in Skagway at that time, because they were all anxious to get maps of the Klondike country so they could see where they were going. No maps of the Klondike existed at that time, but the Australians did not know this and they were directed to a "specialty store" just around the corner and told they might find maps there. The "store" had a specialty, but it wasn't maps, and what happened when a trusting Australian or anybody else entered the place is another story. Usually he came out on his ear a few minutes later and with a warning that he should never again start anything just because he had made a bad guess as to which shell concealed the pea.

Captain Smith employed steerers to direct likely customers to the place, any customer being considered "likely" who had money in his pocket. So it was quite natural that Smith, who was known as Soapy, should employ Smythe, who soon became known as the Hot Cake Kid because that is about all he lived on. Smythe's countrymen were so pleased to find a fellow kangaroo who knew the ropes that they put themselves wholly in his hands, and he took them to where their chances of getting out whole were slim indeed.

Smythe worked on a percentage basis but Smith always had a plausible reason for postponing payday and all the Kid ever got were orders on the Pack Train Restaurant, signed by Soapy and saying "Give him all the hot cakes he wants." In later years, the Hot Cake Kid told the Stroller that if he could collect the percentage due him he could "go back to Austrylia and buy a bloomin' 'ot cyke 'ouse."

But the Hot Cake Kid did not return to Australia, then or ever. After the late Soapy Smith had been laid away, his picking days ended, and his crowd had been dispersed or jailed, Hot Cake went on to Dawson where his skill as a steerer of easy marks found no market at all. In fact, his reception there was extremely cool. Many of his Skagway victims were then in Dawson and some of them had put two and two together. In consequence, when Hot Cake applied for membership in the Sons of the Kangaroo, a fraternal organization then very active in the Klondike, he was overwhelmingly blackballed. He thereupon took to denying his nativity and claiming to have been born and raised in Arkansas, but that also was of short duration. The Amalgamated Brotherhood of Possum Hunters, which also flourished in Dawson, put him through an examination and he described Arkansas as a strip of country joining Pennsylvania on the north and Puyallup on the south.

Thus, when the Stroller came across the Hot Cake Kid in Dawson, the latter was a social outcast, sleeping under the crap tables in the lowest rank of gambling houses and attempting to sustain himself on the soup furnished by those houses to their blackjack boosters. The ingredients of the soup were two gallons of water to one onion and while the resulting product was warming, it was short on nourishment and Hot Cake complained that he was dying of slow starvation. The Stroller took pity on him, staked him to a good square, and using his influence with the owner of the Old Soak Bunkhouse, got him a job as caretaker of the place. This was located, if the Stroller remembers correctly, on Second Avenue between Icicle and All Night Streets and while it advertised under the name Cosmopolitan Hotel it was more generally known by the nickname which derived from the class of patrons it catered to.

Several weeks earlier the owner, a faro dealer at the Monte Carlo, had appealed to the Stroller for advice and assistance because business had been falling off alarmingly at the Old Soak. The place was designed to accommodate a maximum number of patrons—four-bits per night, cash in advance, no refunds under any circumstances—and bunks were tiered four high around the single room. Each night the lower bunks were claimed first and customers who arrived late complained that, having been relieved of four-bits at the door, they couldn't climb to the heights and were forced to sleep on the floor. Many of them were taking their trade elsewhere. Upon learning this, the

Stroller quickly put his inventive genius to work and devised a portable crane which easily lifted even the limpest and groggiest customer to the top bunk. The popularity of the Old Soak was restored.

But the Hot Cake Kid, the Stroller regrets to say, proved a poor caretaker. Although he performed his other duties in a satisfactory manner, he would not oil the crane. Before long it was squealing and shrieking in every sheave and pinion whenever it was used, and since this was always late at night it was an annoyance to all of the people within a block. The thing was declared a nuisance and abated by an Order in Council at Ottawa and the Hot Cake Kid was fired.

It was then that he cleaned his fingernails, bought a white apron and started a bakery, and before long the sun of prosperity began to shine upon him. Flour was then commonly selling in Dawson at $8 for a fifty-pound sack, but an ice jam had backed up the river and flooded a warehouse in which one of the large mercantile companies had stored a hundred tons of flour. Hot Cake bought the lot at two-bits a sack, on jawbone. It proved to be only slightly damaged and when made into bread one small loaf sold for as much as an entire sack had cost. There was no doubt that the Hot Cake Kid knew the baker's trade. He had no trouble selling his product and by the time the entire hundred tons of flour had been worked up Hot Cake had to shovel away the money when he wanted fresh air.

But as so often happens, his fancy lightly turned. He married a dancehall girl known as Flying Kate and only the restrictions of the law prevented his marrying three or four more at the same time. The girls realized, however, that he was not responsible for the law and they did not hold it against him but pitched in to give him what assistance they could in broadcasting his money. It was a business they understood and worked at with a will, and it was not long until Hot Cake's poke was empty. Mrs. Hot then headed south with a dancecaller who had hit seven times straight on the black and the other girls lost interest in him.

And that is about all there is to the story of the Hot Cake Kid. The last time the Stroller heard, he was still around Dawson, making a living, or what passes for a living, by doing a little baking now and then, and still wearing the same old nickname although there are few in Dawson today who know how he came by it. The Stroller will send a copy of the paper containing this story to J. H. P. Smythe in Australia for whatever it may be worth to him, but he does not propose to write a letter to J. H. P. Smythe. The Stroller was never at any time very long on writing letters and he has been mighty short on it ever since one of his love letters was read in court.

MARRIAGE
UP NORTH

IT WAS NOT true, as many believe, that the male population of the North during Gold Rush days was composed almost exclusively of single men and that these men were bachelors by choice. True, many men in the North escaped being led to the hymeneal altar, while dozens if not hundreds of them had left wives and sometimes children behind when they took the gold trail, and for many of these the leave-taking was permanent. But observation spread over a long period has convinced the Stroller that bachelorhood among the yeomanry of the North was a result of necessity rather than choice and that when fortune smiled on a man to the extent that he could support a wife, or thought he could, he lost no time in looking over the eligible field. The fact that the pickings in this field were sometimes slim did not deter him from continuing his prospecting.

The majority of the single men of marriageable age—ninety years and younger—who invaded the North prior to 1900 were then and had for years been drifters. Many were of eastern origin and they had drifted west on attaining manhood and had then worked at many jobs and trades as they wandered from one place to another. Very few of them had much more than a spare pair of socks to show in the way of inventory at the end of any given year. With the discovery of gold in the Klondike, the farm hands, loggers, cowpunchers, clerks and others who were not permanently anchored and were able to round up the price of a ticket and a mackinaw suit headed north. Many of them did not do any better in the Klondike than they had done elsewhere, but others struck six bits to the pan in one way or another, although not necessarily at mining. And as soon as they began to shave on Saturdays and pare their corns preparatory to engaging in the long, juicy waltz at Nigger Jim's, the Monte Carlo or another of the dancehalls, these places constituting the most likely pay streak in the country when matrimony was the object.

And be it known that the female attaches of the dancehalls of that period had little or no antipathy toward being led into matrimony, and as a rule the amount of leading that was required was invisible to the naked eye. In fact, if an ex-logger or ex-cowpuncher did not keep both eyes peeled he was apt to be stumbling up to the altar before he knew what he was up against. And what he was up against was frequently a variety of the bunco game.

The Stroller recalls an instance when a former mule-skinner, after cleaning up a quarter of a million on Hunker Creek, persuaded a fellow he thought was a friend to propose for him, being too bashful to do the job himself. This friend had a lot of fish to fry although he was neither an Izaak Walton nor a short-order cook, and he not only did the proposing but thimble-rigged a swell wedding, with a corpulent actor to impersonate the minister. Of course, the skirted deity was in on the deceit and she modestly promised to love, honor and obey, with the result that for the first time in her checkered career she had the opportunity—and embraced it—to drink all the champagne she could hold. Her capacity was a marvel.

It might be supposed that such an experience would have propelled the victim back to the creeks for a life of celibacy, but it did not. When the man from Hunker Creek learned that he had been jobbed he promptly packed his modesty away in moth balls and boldly began prospecting for a wife. He didn't have to seek either long or far and this time he made sure that the preacher was genuine and the ceremony was legal and aboveboard. But it didn't do him a particle of good because his bride talked him in to taking her and his money outside and there she made the incompatibility of temperament charge stick and the judge awarded her alimony of $500 a month.

Not all of those whose fancies lightly turned, following a clean-up on the creeks or at the faro layout, sought wives in the local dancehalls, though some who did not might have been better off if they had, for by no means all of the dancehall marriages turned sour. More than one lonely miner remembered a former schoolmate whom he had not seen in fifteen or twenty years and a letter or two brought the information that she was either still single or was widowed. Then Jake or Louie or Ole would make a trip to his old home town where he would cut a wide swath in his store clothes and with his stories of riches in the Klondike. A ticket for a double lower would return him and his bride to the coast and soon the ranks of old brides in the Klondike would be swelled by one more. There were more old brides in the country a quarter of a century ago than in any other area of which the Stroller has knowledge. And once the couple was settled, the inevitable reform movement would commence. The Stroller knows a man in whom he was unable to discern a single fault beyond an inclination to occasionally overestimate the value of a small pair, but who was so remodeled and reformed within a few months after his marriage as to be scarcely recognizable. Once marriage set in, the dancehalls saw the new husbands no more and they began changing their shirts oftener than once a month and learned to refrain from chewing tobacco in bed.

While the ninety years the Stroller mentioned earlier as the upper limit of marriageability may have been stretching

170

things a little, it is a fact that age did not seem to be a barrier any more than did an unfortunate appearance or personality. One of the marryingest females the Stroller ever heard of in the North was an old warhorse who operated a combined lodging house and saloon in Skagway. She was constructed along the lines of a battleship and had a disposition to match, together with a foghorn voice and a vocabulary that was the envy of every mule-skinner and dog driver on the White Pass trail. Her first name was Maude and she changed her other name oftener than she changed the blankets in her lodging house, but she was known as Maude the Bouncer from the fact that she did her own bouncing when necessary, in the saloon.

It was in May, 1898, that Maude returned to Skagway aboard the *City of Seattle* from a brief business trip outside and a couple of hours after the steamer docked the Stroller happened to pass her place and was hailed and invited to step inside and name his pizen. Formalities having been observed, Maude said: "Get out your notebook and I'll give you some surprising news. Me and the old gink I met on the boat coming up was married up to the U.S. Commissioner's office a half hour ago. Have another drink and take it out of this private bottle which I keeps for myself."

When asked the name of the fortunate gentleman upon whom she had bestowed her heart and hand, the bride replied, "Well, his first name is Tom, and his second name is Smith or Jones or one of them easy to remember names, but it slips my mind right now. Never mind, though, he just went to the dock to fetch his roll of blankets. Stick around and you can get his name when he comes back.

Taking another jolt from the private bottle, she went on: "This is the fourth marriage for me. None of the other lasted because they didn't have ambition, but I think I've got the right party this time. He's going on into the Klondike and I'm putting up his grubstake. We have it all worked out. He'll stay inside until a year from this fall and then we'll put our combined capital into a nice place outside where we can raise some chickens and a few vegetables. This dump of mine makes good money. There ain't much in renting bunks at fifty cents a night, but since we don't do no laundry there ain't much expense to it, either. But I will say that the fifteen cents for the last drinks comes up mighty fast, and there ain't nothing lost on the first one at ten cents, either. If my husband has any luck at all we should be able to take out twenty thousand bones by a year from next fall."

Just then the "old gink" returned with his blanket roll and his name turned out to be neither Smith nor Jones but Jackson. "Now, see what a nice write-up you can give us in that sheet of yours," said Maude the Bouncer in parting.

It was eight or ten months later that the Stroller ran across Tom Jackson in Dawson. He had a cabin in which he slept but he was sponging his heat in the gambling houses and doing his eating on crackers and cheese at the end of a bar. When asked about the health of his wife in Skagway, he replied:

"Didn't you hear that we busted up two days after we were married? A case of too much ambition, I guess. She gimme some money to buy shoes so's we could call on some of her friends and I thought it would be nice to run it up into a little stake just to show her I was a good provider. A feller told me about a sure thing roulette wheel and when I come home without the shoes or the money, she called me a lot of things which I ain't. That woman has a wonderful command of language. Then she throwed my blankets out into the street and me after 'em."

Five years passed before the Stroller visited Skagway

and by then the town had changed a good deal. Maude's lodging house and saloon had disappeared and even the building had been replaced by a new and modern one. Maude was gone, too, but the Stroller inquired about her and got this reply:

"Maude the Bouncer? Sure I knew her. I guess everybody did. She closed out her business in 1902 and left the country. You remember when the sale of liquor was made legal in Alaska, on July 1, 1899? Well, out of the seventy-five or eighty saloons in Skagway, only eight took out licenses, but quite a few of the little dumps kept right on selling the stuff without a license. Maude was one of them. At first she was pinched every month or so, and then when things tightened up the arrests came every week and the fine imposed was increased for every offense; pyramided, so to speak. It narrowed down to a sort of freeze out game. She swore she would beat the government, and the government saw and raised the ante every time. After she had paid out several thousand dollars in fines, she gave up, took what was left, and beat it. And at that, she had quite a roll. She was married several times after she got rid of Jackson. I don't know how many there were but it seemed like she was up for a divorce every time the District Court sat in Skagway, which was about every four months. None of her husbands lasted more than a day or two, but when she left she told me that after she got settled she intended to have a reunion of all her former husbands. It would be quite a gang. I will say for Maude the Bouncer that she was always improving herself. She never did have any trouble with volume, but she was adding to her vocabulary and working at improving her diction and making her delivery more forcible right up to the time she left."

LOW
WATER

THE WINTER just past was unusually cold and dry, so dry that little snow fell in any part of the vast Yukon Territory. And the cold of winter was followed by a late, slow spring which, when it did finally arrive, came all in a rush. The heavens opened and poured fresh torrents of warm rain and this quickly melted what little snow there was. At long length the ice on the Yukon River broke up, signifying the end of the dreary winter, and the ice, melted snow and rainwater all went booming down the river together in a spectacular and satisfying manner.

At the end of the break-up, the skies cleared, the rains stopped, and the country has since been treated to only an occasional thunderstorm, producing amazing fireworks and lots of noise, but very little in the way of moisture. With no snow left to melt on the hills and no rain in the valleys, the entire country has become exceedingly dry. Rivulets have disappeared completely, creeks have shrunk to trickles, and the water in the Yukon itself has dropped lower and lower.

All of this has caused the residents of the country a great deal of anguish, for this is placer mining country and water is the lifeblood of placer mining. Without it, the whole economy grinds to a halt. The pay dirt, laboriously thawed and hoisted to the surface during the winter months, remains on the dumps, since it cannot be sluiced without water. Unless the pay dirt is sluiced, the gold cannot be recovered and the winter's bills go unpaid. And without payment on the bills, the merchants all get snappish and absent-minded about where they put the lead pencil.

In addition, the lack of water has severely hampered navigation on the Yukon, which is the country's main artery of trade and commerce whether it is liquid in summer or frozen solid in winter. Operators of steamboats have been tearing their hair and using language not heard in refined circles, while the boats, when they have been able to move at all, have frequently stranded on sandbars and stayed there, thus leaving their crews to fight mosquitoes and curse the weather or pray for rain, according to their lights. Even in the deeper sections of the river the steamers have been hitting rocks never before known to exist, and in consequence thereof they have been sinking to the bottom so that grayling and other finny inhabitants of the pools frolic around the engines and through the galleys. And there is nothing more irksome to the owner or captain of a steamboat than to have a grayling peering at its steam gauge or inspecting its boilers.

Old-timers have freely opined that nothing of the kind has ever before happened in the history of the Yukon, and they have called upon the Stroller to back up this opinion. Owners of newspapers are expected to know all and remember all under such circumstances, but the truth is that the oldest of the old-timers has been in the country for only about twenty years while the Stroller has been here ten years, so neither has very much in the way of history to draw upon. But the question came so frequently and so importunely, from old-timers and newcomers alike, that the Stroller was moved last week to try for some first hand information on the subject. In order to do this he visited the Indian camp a short distance below town, taking with him a large flask of his own brand of triple-distilled valley tan for use, if need be, as a lubricant.

There at the camp the Stroller met a long-haired, time-stained son of a storm cloud known as Kawakadada and inquired of him as to the habits of the river and its tributaries in the dim and murky past. The old fellow was disinclined to talk until he spied the flask and then he allowed that he would perhaps take just a drop for his stomach's sake. The "drop" lowered the level in the flask by four fingers, after which Kawakadada opened up. He spoke, of course, in the language of his tribe, but fortunately the Stroller speaks this language fluently and understands it readily, and he here translates the story for the benefit of his readers:

"With the bursting of the present crop of buds, it was mine to gaze for the one hundredth and twenty-seventh time upon the gay and gladsome springtime of the year, and during that time what I ain't seen I reckon ain't worth aseein'.

"You ask if the river was ever so low at this time of year. It was.

"One hundred and four years ago this June the water was much more lowly than at present. I have good cause for remembering that spring, for me and Benchleg Annie were waiting for the sap to run so we could sign articles of agreement, she having won my young and buoyant heart by her prowess at snaring rabbits the previous winter.

"That year there was but seven inches of water on Scatter Bar below town on June 20, and not until the first of July were the canoes able to go to the lake for fish. Tired of waiting for the sap to run, me and Annie forwent the birchbark formality, and it was just as well. That fall she left me for the wigwam of Whomsoever James, he having gone out and killed a moose while I was sitting close to the fire and waiting for a moose to happen by.

"Don't mind if I do. Say, that stuff really hits the spot, doesn't it?

176

"Well, thirty snows then came and went, followed by frolicking spring, before the water was so low again. By that time Woodtick Julia had been drying my salmon, putting mustard plasters on my chest and going through my pockets for a quarter of a century. Julia had long expressed the desire that when she died she be buried on the classic shores of Lake Lebarge, where I first had clasped her salmon-scented form to my manly bosom.

"It was on the 18th of June in 1823 that Julia flopped over and died. And the water was so low that it was the 27th of the following month before the cortege of funeral canoes could proceed to the lake.

"Thanks. You know, this tastes almost like bonded stuff.

"Well, the water remained at a very low stage all that summer and game, fish and berries were all very scarce. But that fall I discovered that Short Sarah had nine bundles of dried salmon cached away and I persuaded her to take me in. Sarah was a good provider and after a few years our wigwam was so full of papooses I had to watch where I stepped and our dogs were all fat and happy. Then came the dry summer of 1853. The water was so low that the salmon could not get up the river and famine stalked rampant. One-eared Charlie killed a caribou and had the only meat in camp. He was a great flirt, made eyes at all the squaws and whispered, 'Plenty of meat in my wigwam.' The squaws ate while the bucks went hungry, same as the dogs, and there was hiyu domestic discord.

"In August of that year Short Sarah, our papooses and all the dogs died of the mange and for a time I was almost driven to rustling my own living. Then Wall-eyed Mary came along and took pity on me. From that time on she has been hanging salmon on my ridge-pole and rubbing my joints with goose-grease, but just between us she sometimes gets very pestiferous. She raises a rumpus every time she sees me wink at another squaw and the younger the squaw the madder she gets. Last week Woodtick Willie gave me a potlatch but she hid my clothes so I couldn't get out.

"Ah! You know, I think this stuff of yours would sell if it got a little of the right kind of promotion.

"Time rolled along just as it is in the habit of doing, and during all the years the waters froze in the fall, only to resume their gay and giddy gurgling with the advent of spring. But the winter of 1872 was very much like the one just past. It was very cold and there was no snow. There was no game, either, and the squaws all went on strike and refused to rustle wood. The bucks held an indignation meeting but the squaws came with clubs and broke it up. They broke some heads, too, and most of the commandments. That was the time Fish Egg Mary opened Scratchy Jack's head with a canoe paddle. She said she caught him robbing her cache of jerked porcupine. That was her story, but the old squaws shook their heads and there was an awful scandal.

"The following spring came in dark, morose and sullen. All Nature wore a frown, and snow-fringed clouds swept restlessly from whither to whence. That June Al Mayo, Tom O'Brien and Nellie Cashman came along and said there was not enough water in the river for a sluicehead, whatever that meant.

"But since that year, the river has done business at the same old stand until the present, but I have me doots about it doing much this year.

"People will probably scorn my advice, as I am but a moth-eaten and frazzled remnant of a once-proud race, but if they were to seek my counsel, I would advise all who wish to winter on the great Outside, of which I wot not, to go no further down the river this year. There will be no water on which to come out again when the sere is on the pumpkin and the fodder's in the shock. As our forefathers used to put it, I have spoken.

"I see there's just a wee drop left and I might as well finish it." The Stroller watched as Kawakadada drained the last four fingers from the flask.

"Don't it beat all how small they make the jugs these days?" The old fellow added. "Come again when you can stay longer and pack more with you. Klahowya."

THE
PANCAKE
KID

EVERY MAILBOAT brings the Stroller from six to a dozen letters from school teachers, sales clerks, office workers, farm girls and other females of assorted ages, sizes and colors. These letters come from every part of the country and invariably the first sentence inquires about opportunities for a job in this part of the world while the next seven paragraphs are devoted to questions about matrimonial prospects in the North.

Ever eager to assist the lowly and downtrodden, whether of the lovelorn variety or otherwise, the Stroller has worked on thousands of these cases over the years, so many of them in fact that he has sometimes been puzzled as to whether he is mainly engaged in running a newspaper or in conducting a combination employment service and matrimonial agency. But the Stroller can state, without tooting his own horn any louder than is merited, that he has been fairly successful both in job placement and in getting rings slipped onto eagerly awaiting fingers.

But a letter received last week, while it followed the general pattern, was one of the most unusual the Stroller has ever received along these lines and presents one of the toughest cases ever thrown in his lap. The letter was postmarked at Eagle, Alaska, a Yukon River town just below the Canadian boundary, and it came from a man, not a woman. All of its several pages were tightly stuck together by a white, gummy substance and this puzzled the Stroller until he was half way through the letter. The writer signed himself "The Pancake Kid" and claims to have been acquainted with the Stroller in earlier years, and this may be true, although the Stroller does not place him. It is clear that this is not the Hot Cake Kid, whom the Stroller did know both in Skagway and Dawson, but another person entirely. And the Stroller will say that he has never received an application that implied greater confidence in his ability to produce the desired result. It was this factor that prompted him to handle the case at all.

The Stroller was about to launch into a description of this Pancake Kid and to list his many qualifications, but on second thought he has decided to print the letter in full. In that way his readers can judge the merits for themselves and each will have an equal opportunity to make the catch. Here is the letter:

Dear Stroller,

Maybe you remember me in Dawson as I was boosting the games around the various places in the years you lived there. Those were the good old days when I never went more than two or three days without eating and the dealer would now and then come across with a new shirt or even a pair of shoes if the suckers were around thick and biting good. After things slowed down and they began adding an extra gallon of water for every onion in the boosters' soup, I quit and got on as porter at the Old Soak Bunkhouse. That was just before you installed that portable crane in the place and there wasn't much to be made there. The customers had mostly been picked pretty clean by the time they got to the Old Soak and I made my eats and that was about all.

I left there the year of the big election campaigns. I guess you must remember that, when there were three campaigns going on all at once, for the Dominion, Territorial and Municipal governments. Both parties and a dozen factions opened headquarters and held continuous open house and a man who could make it from one headquarters to another was in clover. Personally, I was so busy visiting the various headquarters that on election day I forgot to vote. Of course, I wasn't eligible to vote, being nothing but a d—d Yankee, but that wasn't the reason I didn't vote. The truth is that I just plain forgot it.

Things began coming my way when I was made custodian of the spittoons in the Monte Carlo, with the floor pickings as my prerogative. Of course, these pickings were nothing like they had been in the flush times. I remember the time the Kansas City Kid took sick and was hauled off to the hospital and the hospital sent his clothes to the laundry. When they were returned they were accompanied by $39.75 worth of gold dust that had been found in the bottom of the tub when his washing was completed. It was dust that had worked its way into his clothes during the years he slept in the sawdust under the crap tables there at the Monte Carlo. These were the days when no one would stoop to pick up anything under a dollar, but even after I got into the business the pickings would run as high as ten dollars a night despite the fact that some cheapskates would scratch around in the sawdust for as little as a two-bit piece they had dropped. But you had to pay attention to business. One thing was to always to have plenty of sawdust on the floor and another was to keep an eye peeled for chiselers who would buy a short beer and then go shuffling around in the sawdust to see what they could kick up.

Then, just as I was beginning to get a little stake together, the blow fell. The government at Ottawa closed down gambling and as a natural consequence the country began to go to the dogs. Dawson was never the same again and the sawdust at the Monte Carlo or anywhere else wasn't worth the trouble of panning. Things were pretty tough for me. Of course, if I had been an experienced miner I could easily have gotten a job out on the creeks, but the nearest I ever came to mining was once when I got thrown off a freight in Minnesota or somewhere around there and went to work for a week digging potatoes. That was the hardest work I ever ran into, and as mining looked to be just about as hard, I never tackled it.

The next spring I made up my mind to blow out of Dawson and try Nome or maybe the new camp at Fairbanks, so when the breakup came I got aboard an ice cake and started down the river. By the time I passed Eagle my craft was badly honeycombed and crumbling around the edges and when it stuck on a sandbar about four miles below town I came ashore and have been here ever since. At that time it was my ambition to run up a stake and leave the country and I set my sights on $20,000. As time rolled along I lopped off a cypher occasionally and ten years ago I whittled it down to $200 and have been struggling ever since to get that together. The best I have been able to do is $150, which is just enough to get me to Juneau by way of Dawson.

Now, here is what I want you to do for me in Juneau. I want you to scout around and find me a job that will enable me to eat at least two squares a day, with maybe a little extra on the side. A job in a restaurant should be a good bet as I would be sure of my meals that way. I am 49 years old and am a cyclone at washing dishes and rustling wood. If there is a restaurant there that specializes in sourdough bread, I can make myself very useful as what I don't know about sourdough bread hasn't been discovered yet. Also, I am a great hand at sourdough pancakes and my sourdough bucket has never been empty since I landed here twenty-three years ago. So you can see what I mean, I am enclosing one of my pancakes. It won't be as good as it would be hot out of the pan, but it will give you an idea of the texture.

Please let me know right away if you find a job for me, as I want to get out of here before the river freezes up again. I suppose I will see considerable change in Juneau. I was there for three hours when I came north in '98 and it cost me a dollar a minute. When I put my money on red, it came black; when I switched to even, it came odd, and when I played columns, it came up 00 in the green. As I remember it now, everybody I met in Juneau seemed to have an immoderate thirst, but it was not as persistent as the thirst I found when I landed in Skagway where I dropped half of what I escaped from Juneau with in a shell game run by a man they called the Senator. Do you suppose he is still around there? If he is, I might stop and give him a play as I think I have figured out his system.

Say, though, it just occurred to me that you may know a woman there who is looking for a husband. And of course if she should happen to own a restaurant, too, that would be a good selling point as it would be cheaper for her to marry me than to hire a dishwasher. Be sure to call that to her attention. If I have to wash dishes, I want to stipulate that the woman is not to be over 50, but if she has money and I won't have to work I'm willing to stretch the limit ten years or so.

Another thing you should impress upon her is that I am a man of simple habits. I have been living mostly on rabbits and sourdough pancakes and after twenty-three years of that a man is bound to have simple habits. Also, I am very thin. When I stand straight a line from the end of my nose to my toes misses my Adam's apple by less than a quarter of an inch but it misses my waistline by nearly a foot. Find out if she wants me to bring my blankets. If she does, I'll have to wash them and as I have never done this I do not want to start now unless I am sure of coming.

Be sure to let me know right away, and send a picture of her if you can so I'll know what to look for.

Your friend, The Pancake Kid

P.S. Although I am 49, I could easily pass for 65 in case she doesn't want a husband younger than herself.

P.P.S. Be sure to let me know if she wants me to bring my blankets.

Well, there is he, the Pancake Kid, with or without blankets and f.o.b. Juneau. And the fortunate woman who is first in line at the newspaper office to claim him will receive a free pancake turner, compliments of the Stroller.

THE
STROLLER'S
ADVICE
DEPARTMENT

THE STROLLER'S reputation as a dispenser of advice to the lovelorn, the downtrodden, the underdone, has spread to the farthest reaches of the land and as a consequence his mail is laden with requests for liberal helpings of that commodity. Here he shares with his readers — if any — a few of these requests.

* * *

A man who signs himself "Gentlemanly Burglar" complains that owing to the continuous daylight now prevailing, he cannot pursue his calling with any degree of success. He says he has a family to support but that with virtually twenty-four hours of daylight his business is practically at a standstill.

Gent Burg says he left his family down below, expecting to send them a remittance from Wrangell, but found nothing there worth stealing because everyone who had anything had already chased off to the Klondike. So he came on to Dawson and it was here that he encountered the stretched-out days. He says that while he is willing to burgle upon the slightest provocation, no self-respecting burglar will start out to prosecute his calling in broad daylight as it is contrary to professional ethics and that the code of ethics among journeymen burglars is adhered to very rigidly. He also says that robbing clotheslines and shoplifting are not his style.

While there is no long-felt want for an up-to-date burglar here at present, the Stroller may be able to suggest something that will aid Gent Burg:

Locate a couple that has been married about a year and make a deal with the husband to burgle their wedding presents on shares. You steal and sell the bric-a-brac and cut him in on the returns. The Stroller knows of Dawson weddings in which fourteen clocks, eleven carving sets and twenty-one chafing dishes were among the presents. The conglomeration was all right until the space it occupied was wanted for Darling's little bed, but what could be done with it? The owners daren't take it to a junk store and sell it for fear some of the donors might get wise. The usual arrangement, the Stroller is told, is for the husband to get sixty percent, the burglar forty, and in most cases the wife knows nothing about it so the money received by the pater familias can be invested in jackpots and other frivolities.

The Stroller made no charge for this advice, but he believes that if it is followed, Gent Burg can make a living until the nights lengthen and he can go back to practicing his profession by the latest improved methods.

* * *

To Miss Matilda:

You say you are writing the last chapter of a book and you ask me to recommend some reliable publisher who will publish it on commission and not rob you of your share of the profit.

It is evident to me, Matilda, that you have never published a book. There are troubles ahead of you of which you wot not. I do not tell you this to wound your feelings and cause you to weep wet tears, but I do it as a duty, for we literary people must not be mealy mouthed with each other.

You say you will be pleased to confer your book on some deserving publisher. Matilda, there are no deserving publishers. They are as cold blooded as greyling caught through the ice and as ungrateful as a setting hen. Publishers wait for us to call on them and then they make us wish we had gone to live at the poor farm insteading of wearing ourselves out on a manuscript.

Publishers do not appreciate a good thing when it comes their way. For instance, John Bunyan lingered around publishers' homes trampling down their velvet lawns and meek-eyed daisies in his efforts to have his *Pilgrim's Progress* published, but when Dominick McCaffrey finished the last chapter of that coarse, crude book, *The Chambermaid's Own,* he looked out his window to see his front yard full of publishers waiting to grab it.

Those, Matilda, who tear off good solid literature such as I am sure yours is, see few pale pink dots in their horizon and frequently there are holes in their hosiery. It is due to lack of appreciation of true literary talent.

You say, Tilda, you will bring your manuscript to my office some day soon and read it to me. You may bring it to the office, but you will be fleet of foot if you read it to me. In the meantime, I advise you to mail it at once to one of the Juneau papers. They don't publish much but political dope, and I have no doubt that the readers there would greet your product with songs of joy.

* * *

Of the multitude of difficult cases the Stroller has handled during his years as advisor to the lovelorn and downtrodden, one stands out in his mind. Many years ago in Dawson the Stroller received a letter from an unmarried woman in deep despair because, she claimed,

187

she had been unable to corral a husband. Against his better judgment, the Stroller recommended that she come north to Dawson.

It turned out that the woman — the Stroller will call her Jane because that was her name — was not as young as she might have been and was somewhat frayed around the edges. And she was a chronic giggler and simperer, and her every act was kittenish.

The Stroller secured a position for Jane at a roadhouse on Hunker Creek and within three days every single man who had been employed on that creek had jumped his job and was looking for another on Eldorado or Dominion. Jane lasted but a week on Hunker and was once more on the Stroller's hands. He secured another place for her, this time on Bonanza, and in three days she had cleaned that creek as she had Hunker the previous week.

Again she was on the Stroller's hands and this time he secured for her a position as the delivery-window clerk in the postoffice. The month she stayed there the business of the office depreciated forty percent. Men quit writing letters so they would not be required to call at the office for replies. People became aware that the Stroller was responsible for Jane's presence and he began getting letters with skulls and crossbones in the upper corners.

It was the Stroller's move. Something must be done and without delay. Something was done. The Stroller rented a cabin, put a six months' outfit of grub in it, installed Jane as mistress and opened a matrimonial bureau by advertising that a woman with six months' provisons on hand would consider an offer of marriage. Forty proposals were in before the ink on the paper was dry. But thirty-nine of them were too late; the first had been accepted.

The last time the Stroller heard from Jane she was the mother of four and was supporting the family, including the husband, by taking in washing in daylight and baking at night. The Stroller opines that Jane has quit giggling.

* * *

As the time approaches for electing local representatives to the board of the Yukon Council, the Stroller's mail is laden with requests for advice from prospective candidates, all of them asking for information regarding the manner in which a campaign should be conducted.

The Stroller is pleased to be able to impart the desired information, for knowing how campaigns should be conducted is the Stroller's long suit. Acquiring this knowledge has kept him poor, whereas, if he had left politics alone and opened a butcher shop or operated a scavenger wagon he might today have been rich and respected instead of what he is.

In the world of campaigning here are a few pointers that should be heeded:

In the rural districts, such as the outer creeks, wear a dark shirt and blue woolen socks; prefer bacon to beefsteak and enjoy sleeping on the floor. Eat pie with a knife and thereby endear yourself to the common people.

In rural districts the Stroller has found that the following is an excellent campaign decoction:

Two gallons dark, brown swamp water, 4 oz. strychnine, 2 oz. cayenne pepper, 3 oz. gunpowder, 25 or 30 cockroaches and a number of flies. Shake well and add strychnine and pepper as the heat of the campaign increases.

In towns it is best to carelessly approach the bar and say "Step up, boys and name your pizen." By saying "pizen" you won't, in Populist parlance, be accused of being a plutocrat.

Pay marked attention to the children. If the baby's ears are not matched, appear not to notice the deformity. If it looks like a man over on the next claim, be careful not to mention it; such things are apt to happen in a country that imposes a 10 percent royalty. You will never miss it by saying that the baby has the intellecutally shaped head of its pa and the lovely complexion of its ma.

When canvassing this country you won't be asked to hold the calf while the farmer's daughter, who goes around in her bare feet and wears her calico dress like a reefed flag, milks the cow. That is one pleasure you will miss here in the North.

Carry your pockets full of cigars, but smoke a pipe yourself. Cigars with paper rings on them are preferable for the creeks.

In eating boiled potatoes, eat skin and all. It will stamp you as a man who is not stuck up.

Do not speak disparagingly of your opponent in the race, but hint that on the Outside there were two years in which neighbors did not see him, but do not say whether he was in the legislature or the penitentiary. The report will soon get out that it was the latter.

Claim your election with confidence and assert that you will have 500 votes to spare.

After the election if you find you are ingloriously snowed under, take a pick and shovel and hie yourself to the fartherest creek in the district, where you properly belong, instead of boring people by telling them how it happened.

* * *

And Another Jane:

There are times when the Stroller swears a solemn vow to forevermore refrain from working in behalf of the downtrodden, to quit the moral uplift and turn over and go to sleep so far as this cold, clammy and selfish world is concerned. He concludes sometimes that he is wasting

190

his time, that he is a failure and a misfit.

This case also involved a woman named Jane, and it has occurred to the Stroller that his success in the uplift of women with that name has been minimal or lower. It began in Dawson a long time back when the Stroller had more on top and less around the middle than he has now — a lot more and a lot less.

This Jane came from North Dakota and she had heard that the outlying mining districts of the Klondike were full of men who would walk four miles out of their road to see a long stocking hanging on a clothesline. So she came to Dawson and she arrived in the fall when people were banking up their cabins in anticipation of a hard winter.

Someone steered her to the Stroller and she threw both arms around his neck and explained to him her object in invading the Broad White North. It was simple: she wanted a husband and she wanted him soon.

The Stroller had a wide acquaintance on the creeks and knew at least half a hundred men who would take Jane off his hands and ask no questions. In fact, at that time the Stroller had four pigeonholes full of applications for wives. He selected a name at random and sent a note to the fellow, who was known as Mac, asking him to come to town and come in a hurry. The Stroller had Jane stashed in a lodging house and wanted to unload her before the neighbors began to talk.

The fellow arrived in time to get a shave and haircut before time for the little dinner the Stroller had arranged, with plates for three and Jesse Moore for two. Jane didn't drink.

Next morning there was a quiet wedding and that afternoon Jane returned with her liege lord to his cabin on Bonanza Creek to boil beans, build sourdough bread and fry hots. For several months the Stroller received a letter from Jane every week and they were full of such expressions as "cup of joy slopping over," "bustin' with happiness" and the like.

A year later the Rev. John Pringle officiated at the christening of a boy baby on Bonanza and the initials of his front name were E.J.W. Jane wrote that she needed a go-cart to push her happiness around in. Then the Stroller moved to Whitehourse to continue his uplift work in the southern Yukon and still later he moved to Douglas which needed it even more. He lost track of the family he had been instrumental in organizing, but Jane did not lose track of the Stroller because this week he received a letter that brought him up with short turn. It was as follows:

Gold Bottom, Y.T., September 27

Despised sir:
You will no doubt be salivated (Jane was always extravagant in the use of words) to hear from me. For the past ten years my heart has been as cold as a dead fish and I hain't smiled in longer'n that. Mac never speaks to me except to jaw me and he never comes home at nite if there is a roadhouse open within four miles of our cabin. When he does come he is always soaked to the neck. He hain't kissed me since 11 year ago Christmas and then I would have sooner kissed the bunghole of a beer kag.

And you are responsible for all my woe. You could have picked the name of some better man out of that pigeonhole if you had cared to. At any rate, you could not have pulled a wuss one. The trouble between me and Mac started when I made him a shirt nigh on 11 year ago. He swears he has been warped ever since he tried to put it on. Now he says he will give me enough money to take us, myself and your puny namesake, outen the country this fall. We start next week and will stop in your town and visit you until after Christmas. I have a heap to tell you.

Yours in misery and calico,
Jane

After reading the letter the Stroller paid a Juneau lawyer $7.50 to send a wire to Jane to head her off, signing his name as administrator of the Stroller's estate. The lawyer admitted to the Stroller in confidence that it was the biggest fee he had collected since the war broke out, so some good has come of it.

* * *

No. 32 Above, Hunker
Dear Stroller:
I see in your paper that the police are now giving out blue tickets and since I want to get back to Webfoot, Oregon, this fall and the clean-up does not look too promising, a free ticket even as far as Whitehorse would help. How can I get one.
Hunker

Dear Hunker:
Start early some morning and patronize evey roadhouse bar between 32 Above and the Dawson police headquarters. If you do not have a good case when you start, you will have when you arrive and the Stroller guarantees you will receive distinguished consideration at the hands of the police. It may be in the form of a blue ticket or it may be a saw and a pile of cordwood, but rest assured that you will not draw a blank.

* * *

Mr. Stroller, Whitehorse:
I write to inquire if there is an opening at your town for a young man of my attainments and qualifications. I am a bright and shining light in society, my specialty being imparting to less favored young men the happy art of appearing in the company of young women at dinner parties, balls, and etc. in good form and without appearing as a chump. For the privilege of associating with me and the profit derived from such association I would expect each young man to pay me about $10 per month.
If there is an opening there for me, and early answer will oblige.
H. Carrington F. Johnson

Whitehorse, January 4

To: H. Carrington F:

Had you searched from Cape Horn to north of Herschel Island you could not have selected a point with such a fine opening for yourself. Hasten hither when spring comes, H. Carrington F., and you will confront the opening soon after your arrival. It is situated only a short distance above town and is called Miles Canyon, it has a constant yearning for young men such as you describe yourself.

Please change your socks at Skagway on the way in so as not to impair the purity of our drinking water.

If your people desire you for obsequies, they should arrange to meet you with drag hooks at St. Michael sometime next summer.

So long, H. Carrington F.

STROLLER

* * *

INDIAN
LORE

WHEN THE Stroller moved from Skagway in Alaska, to Dawson in Yukon Territory, he began to hear a good deal about the lore of the Indians with regard to weather. Dawson is the center for the Klondike placer mining country and placer miners have a vital interest in the weather and especially in the snowfall of winter and the rainfall of summer, as the success of their operations depends heavily upon an adequate and continuous flow of water during the summer months. Weather records were all but non-existent in the Klondike at the time since by far the greater part of its white population had been there for less than a year and only a handful of white men had been in the country for as long as ten years. The Indians had been there long before the white men showed up, of course, and as a result the expression "according to the Indians" was much used in commenting on present weather or discussing what to expect in the line of meteorology.

The Stroller at that time took little stock in this Indian weather lore, considering it no more reliable than the weather lore of the white man. For the Stroller has observed that while the weather is a subject of intense interest everywhere, on no subject is man's memory shorter or more likely to be at fault. Almost every winter that comes along is asserted to be the coldest or the mildest or to have produced the heaviest fall of snow, just as nearly every summer is cited as the hottest or the shortest or the wettest in the memory of man. While he was at Dawson, however, the Stroller's time was occupied by many other matters and he took the weather pretty much as it found him, protected by a parka and ear-muffs or a rubber coat, as conditions might dictate.

Later on the Stroller moved from Dawson to Whitehorse in the southern Yukon and there things were more leisurely and he found time to pursue his interests in anthropology, archaeology, alchemy (with special attention to what could be done with rye) and weather, upon all of which subjects he now recognizes himself as an authority. And in the course of these studies the Stroller consulted frequently with members of the Lebarge tribe of the Stick Indians, who live in that part of the country. When questions of history and early weather phenomena arose, as they often did, the oldest member of the tribe, Kawakadada, was helpful. At the age of 128 years he still had a retentive memory and he would turn it loose when suitably encouraged. The stroller always carried a large flask of encouragement when on such quests. And it was from Kawakadada that the Stroller first learned of the Birch Bark Book. It happened this way:

One morning early in July the Stroller awoke to find an inch of frost on the windowpanes and ice covering every pond in the vicinity. Hastily digging his winter garb out of the closet and donning it, the Stroller repaired at once to the Indian village to consult Kawakadada and learn when a heavy freeze had last occurred so late in the season. He found the old fellow shivering under a pile of moth-eaten blankets and directing his current wife to chuck more wood on the fire and to hurry up about it. But so far as history was concerned, Kawakadada was uncommunicative that morning and even the usual treatment, a jolt of the Stroller's best hand-made extract of rye, failed to limber his tongue. He grunted something

196

to the effect that "he couldn't be expected to remember everything" and that he would "have to look at the book". He then instructed the Stroller to return in two days "if it warms up," and burrowed down into his blankets.

The Stroller assumed that the reference to "the book" was merely a figure of speech, but on his next visit he learned that there was indeed a book. As it has no title, he has labeled it the Birch Bark Book, as its many pages are of birch bark. It has been handed down from generation to generation through the male side of the Boss family and in it is recorded the history of the tribe for more than a thousand years, together with suitable comments on the weather, politics, business conditions and the state of the nation. Long negotiations, which he will not detail here, brought the book into the Stroller's hands and he has since been occupied with translating it from the Indian language into English. Of course there are those who assert that the North American Indians have no written language, but the very existence of the Birch Bark Book discloses their ignorance. It is the Stroller's intention to bring out his English translation as soon as he can locate a publisher for it, as it is his opinion that this will be the greatest publishing event since Johann Gutenberg put the Bible in type, although to date no publisher has shared this opinion.

In the meanwhile, the Stroller is printing here a few of the entries from the book. This will accomplish two things: it will give his readers a sampling of the contents of this remarkable volume, and it will help fill the columns of this week's issue of the paper, columns which would otherwise have to be filled with Aunt Sophie's receipe for sourdough prune cake and the Stroller's own home remedy for ingrown hangnails. Here are the entries as freely translated by the Stroller, starting with the very first one in the book:

December 31, 876 — Year ends about average. Good run of salmon and plenty dried fish in the cache, but ice worm crop looks like a failure. Unrest reported in Saskatchewan and Ireland, but otherwise quiet on the international scene.

September 24, 1000 — Cold all summer. Fish very poor, mostly mouth and backbone. hard winter ahead. Leif Ericson landed on the East Coast. This place going to be overrun with Squareheads if we don't watch out.

July 18, 1228 — All berry blossoms killed by June frost. No berries for grouse, no grouse for people. Dogs poor, too tough to either boil or fry. People hungry and moth-eaten, but Genghis Khan is dead so we don't have to worry any more about him.

June 6, 1431 — Ice all gone. First canoes started down the river for fishing. Looks like warm summer. Got word Joan of Arc burned at stake last week. Them white people, always thinking up something new. Good idea. Save it for future reference.

August 14, 1492 — Dry summer. Hardly any water in river. Everybody got mange. No salmon showed up yet. Columbus has sailed for our shores. Big pow-wow to discuss sending delegation to meet him. Decided against it after Whomsoever Will pointed out that Columbus don't know where he's going and it's not our business to tell him where he is when he gets here.

January 7, 1561 — Coldest winter since 983. Ground froze one squaw deep in October, two squaws deep in November. Blue snow falls every day. Plenty eats, though. Ice worms everywhere. Some grow twenty inches long. Snowbirds eat ice worms, get big as grouse. Hiyu good eating.

November 4, 1607 — Rain, rain, rain. Worse than Noah's time. Can't keep nothing dry. Dried salmon get moldy, dried ice worms from last winter turn sour. Everybody wear grouch, especially squaws! We hear Captain John Smith starting settlement at Jamestown. This country getting overcrowded.

October 10, 1626 — Hard times all over. Cold wind blow all June, ice in July, sleep 'em close in August. Everybody wear hairy side in. No sap in either trees or tribe. Stock market on skids, real estate values shot. Injuns sell Manhattan Island for $24 worth of junk jewelry. Glad we don't have to pay taxes.

September 18, 1638 — Good times this year. Plenty berries, hiyu salmon, lots of moose. Dogs and papooses fat and happy. Squaws fat. Two shiploads of Swedes landed in Delaware to start a colony. Sent party to trade moccasins and beadwork to 'em for snoose.

July 22, 1741 — No summer yet. Ground all froze. Grouse eggs freeze on bottom side, hatch on top side only. Young grouse all lopsided, fly crooked. Hard to catch. Young squaws leery about taking bucks to support. Social life much disorganized. Captain Bering sighted the coast last week. Didn't know where he was. Didn't send nobody to ask us, so let him find out for himself.

September 14, 1751 — Woe is us. No rain all summer. No berries, no grouse, no fish, no balms in Gilead, no eats in whole country. On top everything else, white man changes calendar. Eleven whole days dropped. All mixed up on anniversaries. Why don't white man stay home, leave things alone?

December 17, 1773 — No moose in hills, no grouse, no rabbits, no nothing. Hardly that. Shiver in October, blue snow in November. Everybody cold. Fat squaws who been in discard for years now popular. King George's tax collector got froze in at Carcross. Good place for him! Squaws hear about Boston Tea Party, want to hold one here. Bucks point out have to cut hole in ice to dump tea.

Too much work. Squaws do war dance, talk about taxation without representation. Crazy squaws. Got no tea anyway.

July 5, 1776 — Cold as winter. Ice hasn't gone out yet. Looks like nobody win ice pool this year. No fish. Hiyu rabbits but very skinny. Gaunt famine stalks the land. Declaration of Independence adopted in Philadelphia yesterday. Oh, well, let 'em go. We still got the Klondike.

December 26, 1776 — Everything mixed up. No summer, now no winter. Mild. No ice worms. No snow to track moose. No ice on river to fish through. No end to summer scratching. Mange spreading. All cockeyed. Must be all them cannons they're shooting off in the Revolution that's doing it. Moccasin telegraph brings word Washington crossed the Delaware last night. More ice in Delaware than in Yukon.

June 20, 1837 — Summer early this year. Lots of berries. Plenty grouse. Plenty troubles, too. Queen Victoria takes throne today. Squaws all get uppity, say things be different now. Refuse to pick berries or rustle wood. Want new clothes for Coronation Ball. God bless the Queen, but what's this country coming to?

January 30, 1848 — Snow every month for nineteen months in a row now. Jerked porcupine at a premium. Desolation and bony dogs stalk rampant through the village. everybody sleep in community bed to keep warm. Not so bad at that! Gold discovered down at Sutter's Mill in California. Better keep mum about Klondike.

October 18, 1867 — Plenty salmon and moose, but bad depression otherwise. Russians dumped Alaska on market at two cents an acre. Real estate worthless. bottom fell out of stock market. Consolidated Ice Worm Preserving Co. common fell to 6-3/4 with no takers. Brokers all looking for fourteen-story trees to jump out of.

December 11, 1869 — Heavy snow, much cold. Everybody sleep with heads under blankets. Phew! Much troubles. Legislature in Wyoming territory passed woman's suffrage bill yesterday. Tried to keep news from squaws. No luck. Big Mouth John let it slip. Scalped him.

September 14, 1875 — Hiyu salmon in river. Everybody busy catching and drying for winter. George Holt come through in August. First white man to cross Chilkoot Pass. Old people shake heads, say he won't be the last. Sure enough, next week WCTU representative arrives with suitcase full of white ribbons. Organizes squaws. They all take hatchets and bust up stills. Bucks organize, too. Catch WCTU representative. Tried out that Joan of Arc stunt. Worked good.

May 29, 1876 — Looks like good summer coming. Geese show up early, ahead of game wardens, so we do pretty good. Recruiting sergeant arrives from Sitting Bull's camp. Claims they going after General Custer next month, needs more troops. Young bucks eager to enlist but wiser heads prevail in interest of international harmony.

August 20, 1896 — Summer started off good but now all turned sour. That Skookum Jim can't keep a secret. Went and showed George Carmack where to find gold down on Rabbit Creek. Much excitement. White men rushing everywhere. This used to be good country. Now what? Old people shake heads, point to California. Gold found there, now whole place cultus. They say same thing happen here. Injun better give up. Oh, well, after while gold all gone, maybe white people go, too. Give country back to Injuns.

JOHN HENRY
LITTLEJOHN

Life isn't in holding a good hand,
but in playing a poor hand well.

AFTER SITTING in front of his typewriter for half an hour in a vain effort to dream up something to write about to fill out this week's paper, the Stroller noticed the above lines on the bottom of a calendar and they started him to thinking, something he seldom does because thinking causes wrinkles. And while he was thinking, his mind wandered back through dim vistas of the past until it came to John Henry Littlejohn, and there it stopped.

John Henry Littlejohn was an Englishman and he left his ancestral home early in 1898 for the Klondike. John Henry knew "Lunnon" but he didn't know much else and he spoke of Americans as "uncouth" and of Canadians "bloomin' Colonials," with the result that both Americans and Canadians handed John Henry various, diverse and sundry packages.

When John Henry left England he had money in every pocket. He was separated from a considerable portion of it in Vancouver and from there he went to Seattle where they saw him coming and arranged to annex another section of his roll.

The Stroller and John Henry Littlejohn traveled from Seattle to Skagway on the same little wooden steamer and it was on the morning of the second day out of Seattle that the attention of the Stroller was first drawn to the

Englishman. The latter was flipping silver dollars on the upper deck with a fellow who came from Brooklyn and who had suggested a game of "Heads I win, tails you lose." Needless to say, the Brooklynite made his fare north at that session. That same afternoon the Stroller flipped a few coins with John Henry just to illustrate to him that he had been bucking a sure thing game. And when the light finally dawned on John Henry, his only comment was, "Deucedly clever, don't you know!"

But it was at Skagway that John Henry really began to bump the bumps. There he fell in love with Little Poketa who was a member of a team of rope artists appearing at Clancy's Music Hall. The other member of the team was known as Iron Jaw and his specialty was dangling from a rope by his teeth and swinging far out over the audience with Little Poketa hanging to his heels. John Henry and Little Poketa hoisted a few at the conclusion of her act on the first night he saw her and when she confided to him that she was tired of show life and yearned for domesticity, he kindly offered to marry her. His generosity was appreciated to the extent that his offer was tentatively accepted, the tentative feature being that he must wait until the engagement at Clancy's was fulfilled.

Little Poketa said also that she would like a diamond ring to make the other janes jealous, and the diamond ring and other attentions were bestowed and champagne suppers at the Pack Train Restaurant became almost nightly occurrences. John Henry did have a little trouble in understanding why Little Poketa insisted on taking Iron Jaw with them to their midnight suppers, but she explained that her contract with her stunt partner explicitly stated that when one of them had a chance to partake of a champagne supper, the other must be in on it. Moreover, she said, Iron Jaw had taken a great liking to John Henry and enjoyed his company. Iron Jaw was also very pleased

203

that his little partner had been so fortunate as to win a man of John Henry's stability and prospects, and he wished them long life, prosperity and wedded bliss. The future indeed bore a roseate tint for John Henry.

Finally came the last night of the rope act at Clancy's and the wedding was to take place at 4 o'clock the following afternoon. John Henry was exceedingly happy and little birds warbled from the ridgepole of his heart. Just what warbled in his head the Stroller does not know, but whatever it was warbled him into inviting the entire cast at the Music Hall to make merry with him that night at the Pack Train. This they did, to the number of a couple of dozen. Five cases of champagne were in evidence until the evidence disappeared; corks popped musically, and the true inwardness of a score of young Plymouth Rocks was discussed and explored at the festal board. All the other show people had been informed of the approaching wedding and many were the felicitations bestowed on the happy man who was paying the bills. It was a great night and the dawn of the new day was peeping before John Henry slept.

It was about 2 o'clock in the afternoon when he awoke; just time for a bawth, rubdown and shave and to dress for the big event at 4 o'clock. It was about 3:30 when he entered the hotel lobby and the clerk handed him a letter which he immediately opened. It read:

Mr. John Henry Littlejohn,

You may be interested to know that Little Poketa has been my wife for nine years and that we have four children whom we farmed out with relatives in Seattle when we came north a month ago to fill the engagement at Clancy's. This is being written at 10 a.m. as we leave on the *Al-Ki,* sailing for Seattle at noon. Hope you are enjoying your sleep as much as we have enjoyed your hospitality during the past three weeks.

Respectfully,
Iron Jaw
P.S. Your supper last night was a pippin.

"My word," exclaimed John Henry Littlejohn when he had digested the contents of the letter.

Three years then rolled by. The Stroller was living in Dawson and was on his way to report a political convention at the town of Caribou on Dominion Creek. The temperature was forty degrees below zero, it was forty-five miles from Dawson to Caribou, and the stage horses were staggering when the Midway Roadhouse was reached. There the passengers crawled from under their fur robes and entered the roadhouse for lunch. After lunch, when the charcoal footwarmers had been replenished and the passengers were bundling themselves into their coats and robes, the Stroller happened to glance at the porter who was carrying armloads of wood into the building. It was John Henry Littlejohn and he, realizing that he had been recognized, came over and said, "I was in hope that you had forgotten me."

Two days later, on the return trip, the Stroller stopped and had a long talk with John Henry. The latter confided that he had made a "bloomin' fool" of himself in Skagway and had spent $2,000 in three weeks, including the cost of the diamond ring. "She was a swell looker," he added, wistfully, and went on to say that the part he regretted most was the quantity of champagne Iron Jaw had consumed at his expense.

John Henry said he had spent the last of his money getting to Dawson and when he tried to recoup his fortune by tossing coins, "Heads I win, tails you lose," with a crude American, the latter had promptly knocked him

205

down. John Henry just could not seem to make a hit in Dawson and he had finally welcomed the opportunity to take the position at the Midway Roadhouse where he carried wood and water for his board, room and occasional drink. Sometimes it was semi-occasional. To make matters worse, he said, some busybody had written to his people in England about his actions at Skagway and they had stopped his allowance, although John Henry called it his patrimony. He requested the Stroller to send him a copy of the London Times if one could be located around Dawson.

The story of John Henry Littlejohn might have ended right there and it would not have been greatly different than that of hundreds of others who drifted into the North during the Gold Rush and became derelicts there. But there was more to John Henry's story, and to end it now would not be fair to him.

A few months after the Stroller saw John Henry at the Midway Roadhouse he moved a short distance down Hunker Creek and took a position as bartender for a woman who was conducting a roadhouse. This roadhouse was on a claim the woman had located herself but on which no paystreak had ever been found, although she had not given up looking for it. And, being a thrifty woman, she put John Henry to work sinking a prospect hole back of the house whenever he was not busy at the bar. At ten feet he found colors and at twenty feet he struck two dollars to the pan. But he kept the find to himself until he had proposed to the woman and been accepted, she reckoning that it was cheaper to marry her bartender than to pay him wages. Had she turned him down, John Henry intended to continue sniping $40 or $50 worth of gold from the shaft every day, as he had been doing for a month before he proposed, as he had developed a great longing to return to dear old London.

As soon as they were married, John Henry announced the discovery and they opened a bottle of champagne, the last one his wife would let him open in the North. Three years later, having worked out their property and sold the tailings to the Guggenheims, Mr. and Mrs. Littlejohn left the North for England, stopping off in Seattle for a month on the way. And there in Seattle John Henry ran across Iron Jaw, who was swamping at the Horseshoe Saloon, the rope act having lost its crowd-stopping popularity. So every day, and sometimes several times a day, John Henry dropped around to the Horseshoe Saloon and sat at the bar and drank champagne. And when he saw Iron Jaw around with his mop and bucket or juggling the spittoons, he would call out to him, "I say, my good man, won't you have a pony beer? I don't suppose you've ever tasted champagne." And after John Henry tired of that, the couple went on to England where, so far as the Stroller knows, they are living happily ever after.

So, after all, while John Henry Littlejohn once held a good hand and played it very poorly, he later held a poor hand and played it well.

THE STROLLER'S LAST BURGLARY

FOR SALE — Complete set of Burglars' Tools, slightly rusty through lack of use, but all in good condition. Will open anything except a YMCA convention. Apply to the Stroller.

FOR THE PAST eight years the Stroller has been threatening to insert the above advertisement, and only sentiment engendered by long association and ownership has prevented his doing so. It will be eight years this fall since the Stroller last used his burglars' tools. Previous to that time he frequently engaged in the sensational and pleasantly thrilling occupation of breaking into rooms when all Nature was wrapped in the long, unstarched robe of slumber. It required considerable resolution for him to break away from this long established custom, as it had become sort of second nature.

The Stroller was always of an easy-going disposition and he early acquired the habit of taking things as he found them, a habit which he followed with more or less success until the experience which he is about to relate came to him eight years ago. He was then operating in a certain town in the southern Yukon where many people with fat pokes and heavy purses were wont to stop for a day or a night while on their way outside from the Interior. Business had been good all fall and the Stroller was adding to his bank account after the arrival of nearly every steamer from the lower river. He was prospering and was seriously considering running for office at an early date when his conscience overtook him after lingering several laps behind for a long period of years. It was this way:

Being at the wharf when a steamer landed and the passengers swarmed down the gangplank, the Stroller spotted a fat handbag and followed it to one of the local hotels. The hotel register showed to which room the owner of the heavy bag was assigned, but evidently some kind of a trade was made, for that night when the Stroller entered the room with the help of his kit of tools, there was no sign of the bag. Moreover, the man on the bed did not look, when the rays of the dark lantern were thrown on him, as though he had ever been in contact with half a dozen ounces of gold dust in his life. But having learned by long experience at burglary that appearances are deceiving, the Stroller decided to take stock of the stranger's belongings.

From beneath the pillow was extracted a long but somewhat lean wallet which showed evidence of having seen better days. It was tied around by a greasy cotton string and on being opened and its contents examined it was found to contain $115 in cash, a ticket to Skagway, a receipt for making hootchinoo, and a long diary covering a period from January, 1898, to the present. Transferring the cash to his own pocket and hastily copying the hootch receipt for future reference, the Stroller focused the light of his lantern on the diary and proceeded to read that which was to decide him in the matter of advertising his burglars' tools for sale.

The diary had not been religiously kept, some of the

entries being as much as six months apart, but the following are some of the notations:

Squash Hollow, Missouri, Jan. 17, 1898 — Leave today for the Klondike. Have $500. Nan has promised to wait for me if I will return in two years.

Seattle, Jan.. 24 — Met a stranger who said he owns rich claims near Dawson, and hired out to him for $10 per day, wages to start at once. He is also to pay my way to Dawson. Loaned him $50 until the bank opened. That was yesterday and I have not seen him since.

Seattle, Feb. 5 — Have given up ever seeing the stranger to whom I loaned $50. He probably fell in the bay and was drowned. Too bad, because he seemed like a nice fellow. I leave for the North tomorrow.

Skagway, Feb. 15 — Landed here last night. A man named Soapy Smith took me to his office to show me a map of the Klondike. While there I was introduced to a game played with three little shells. It cost me $85.

Big Salmon, March 20 — Am this far on the way to Dawson. Have pulled a handsled all the way from Skagway. A girl named Gum Boot Kitty rode on my sled nearly all of today. What would Nan think?

Dawson, May 2 — Reached here yesterday after a hard trip. Go to work tomorrow on Bonanza at $9 per day and board. Kitty got a job dancing at Nigger Jim's.

Cheechako Hill, Oct. 10 — Have worked all summer and am $745 to the good. Will take a trip to Dawson tomorrow.

Dawson, Oct. 12 — Reached town yesterday. Had a few dances last night and this morning ate crackers off the end of Tom Chisholm's bar for breakfast. Am flat broke. Will send home the next money I get. Kitty has married Swiftwater Bill.

Dawson, May 1, 1899 — Worked and loafed alternately through the winter. Boosted at a blackjack game for eating money. Like boosting better than mining.

Dawson, Oct. 20 — Last boat has left for the Outside and I am still here. Nan sends love and says my two years is nearly up. She probably thinks I am a millionaire. Poor Nan.

Dawson, April 13, 1900 — Have been running a crap game since last fall. My credit is good, so I am always in the hole.

Dawson, Sept. 15 — Nan writes that Bill Woods has a team of mules and a breaking plough. Bill was always stuck on Nan.

Dawson, June 4, 1901 — Am making a precarious living bucking faro. Uncle Hoffman is camping on my trail.

Dawson, Jan. 10, 1902 — A scorching letter from Nan. Bill Woods is building a house.

Dawson, Aug. 4 — Letter from home says Nan and Bill Woods are married. The letter came a week ago. Have been drunk ever since.

Dawson, March 1, 1903 — An order from Ottawa has closed gambling here. Me for the Tanana.

Fairbanks, Dec. 12 — This is not the town Dawson used to be. The fools don't bet their money like we did in Dawson. My health is failing and I'm near down and out.

Fairbanks, Oct. 7, 1904 — Having a job as swamper in a saloon. I tend bar two hours every morning and am striving to knock down enough to get out of the country next summer.

Fairbanks, June 5, 1905 — Have just completed six months for rolling a drunk. Wish I was back in Missouri.

Fairbanks, March 4, 1906 — Am still in Fairbanks and only the Lord and myself know how I live. Oh, for a square!

Fairbanks, Nov. 15, 1906 — The close of navigation left me still here. Haven't written or heard from home for four years.

Fairbanks, June 8, 1907 — Am almost a wreck. Don't know what condition my stomach is in as it rarely gets a chance to demonstrate its condition.

Fairbanks, Jan. 14, 1908 — This is the hardest winter I have yet experienced. All the old push has left and there are none to hand me the price.

Fairbanks, Oct. 30 — The close of navigation finds me in the Fairbanks hospital, the best place I have been for a long time. Hope it lasts until spring.

Fairbanks, July 12, 1909 — There is a movement on foot to raise money to send me out this fall. The movement has my best wishes for its success.

Fairbanks, Sept. 15 — The movement has moved and I am to leave Fairbanks this evening for the Outside by way of Dawson.

Dawson, Sept. 26 — The old town don't look like it did when I was investing my dust in left alamans. Nobody seems to know me and if they do they look on me as a white check. Nearly twelve years ago I arrived here in the vigor of young manhood, the nightingale of blissful anticipation roosting high on the ridgepole of my heart, which was lighted with the rays of hope and future happiness. Today I am a mere hulk of my former self — lost to Nan, lost to my family, lost to my self-respect and, I fear, lost to God.

As the Stroller read the final entry in the diary, a tear coursed its way down his nose, trembled there for a moment, then took a header into space. Near him on the bed was the author of the diary. From the interior realms of his raiment the Stroller extracted the $115 he had appropriated to himself. It was carefully replaced in the timeworn wallet, accompanied by another twenty which the Stroller had stealthily removed from the pocket of a man as the crowd surged around the hotel register earlier that day. The greasy cotton string was carefully tied around the wallet and it was replaced under the pillow. The Stroller then quietly moved from the room, relocked the door, and silently descended the stairs. On his way down he met another popular and influential local burglar, to whom he wished success, but whispered in his ear: "Don't bother the fellow in No. 23. The poor devil has nothing left but his record."

THE BLUEBERRY PIES OF DOUGLAS

THE STROLLER has eaten pie in Florida made from sweet potatoes, and it was good. He has eaten iceworm pie in the shadow of the north pole, and it was good. Between those widely different terminals he has eaten all kinds and conditions of pie, some of which was good and some of which was better.

From the pearly shores of the Atlantic to the blue waters of the Pacific the old-fashioned apple pie of our forebears holds first place in many households. From the icebound lakes of the North to the placid bosom of the Gulf of Mexico the mince pie is revered. In New England the pumpkin pie is placed on a pedestal and worshipped.

But of all the pies ever concocted, built, perpetrated or prepared, the blueberry pie of Douglas, Alaska, is pre-eminently the top liner. In the final roll of pie honor it will stand out as overshadowing and eclipsing any and everything ever attempted in the pie line.

In connection with the preceding paragraph the Stroller wishes to go on record as boldly asserting — without fear of gainsay or successful contradiction — that the women of Douglas are the best blueberry pie bakers in all this land.

Some doubting Thomas may here interrupt with, "How does the Stroller know so much about the attainments of the women of Douglas as bakers of blueberry pie?" He will elucidate.

Previous to this week and since the opening of the blueberry season the Stroller was shy a pie baker of his own, but he was not shy the pie. In the largeness of their hearts the women of the town kept the Stroller supplied with blueberry pie and he would be an ingrate did he not thank them for their kindness and highly appreciated thoughtfulness.

Sweet little girls with pigtails neatly tied in ribbon would gently tap at the Stroller's door and hand in something neatly done up in paper, with the message, "Mother sent you this." it would be blueberry pie. Boys, bright-eyed, but with mud-spattered clothes, would loudly proclaim at the same door, "Hey, here's sumpin' for you." It would be blueberry pie. The result was that the Stroller kept blueberry pies in the oven to keep them hot, and he kept blueberry pies in the ice box to keep them cold. He ate blueberry pie for breakfast, lunch and dinner and the last thing before retiring at night. At least twice during the night he would get up and eat a quarter of a blueberry pie — sometimes a half. No bear that ever roamed the primeval forest had anything on the Stroller in the line of blueberries.

"COUNT"
CARBONNEAU

"COUNT CARBONNEAU? Did you say Count Carbonneau?" said Mr. Justice Dugas one day to the Stroller. "You can publish it over my signature that he is no more a count than you or I.

"Why, the last time I met him was a year ago in Montreal. I was a magistrate then and he came to me as per ordinance to secure a saloon license. You can put that, too, over my signature if you like. He's French Canadian; there is no title of count belongs to him at all. Quote me as your authority, for knowing him as I do, I should feel that possibly I was slightly to blame if by the assumption of this title he was enabled to mislead anyone."

Those are the words, exactly as the Stroller wrote them, in his column in *The Klondike Nugget* in Dawson just twenty years ago. That item appeared, in fact, on November 15 in the year 1899.

The Stroller did not pay great heed to the words of Mr. Justice Dugas for the reason that at least half of the people who had arrived in the Klondike by then were trying to remember what name they had given the Mounted Police at Tagish or had cricks in their necks from looking over their shoulders to see whether they were being followed. But every now and then, over the years, the Stroller has remembered those words.

Charles Eugene Carbonneau arrived in Dawson before the Stroller did, sometime in the summer of 1898. He

216

represented European capital, the Anglo-French Klondike Syndicate or some such name. He bought a claim on Bonanza Creek and another on Eldorado and put some men to work. Two of the four Dawson newspapers always put his title in quotation marks when they had occasion to refer to him and it was not taken very seriously.

Dawson did not take him seriously, that is, until the fall of 1900 when he married Miss Belinda Mulrooney, proprietor of the Fairview Hotel, owner of several mining claims, and reputedly the richest woman in the Klondike. Whether she was the richest or not the Stroller does not know, but she undoubtedly outranked Carbonneau in that department.

Miss Mulrooney had reached Dawson in the early summer of 1897 and had built a reputation as a shrewd, hard-driving business woman. It was said that she chewed tobacco, could swear like a mule-skinner and was capable of violent action. The latter was evidenced by the fact that she ended a dispute with one mine owner by bashing him over the head with a shovel, and some years later she horse-whipped a banker who had offended her.

On the other hand, Belinda Mulrooney was widely known for her philanthropies, and she acted as sort of mother hen to a large family including her parents and several sisters and brothers. Just why the shrewd Belinda fell for a montebank like Carbonneau was one of the great mysteries of the North.

But the knot was tied by Father Demerais in Dawson's St. Joseph's Church in October, 1900, and the newly-weds headed for the mines east of town. According to bits of news that drifted into the newspapers, Belinda operated a claim on Eldorado very successfully, with a big clean-up the following summer. But over on Bonanza, Carbonneau did poorly. His mine flooded, there was a cave-in and a miner was killed, the operation was shut down for a time by the mining inspector for safety reasons. Whether it was bad luck or sheer ineptitude the Stroller does not know, although he has an opinion.

In the fall the Carbonneaus left for a high-stepping honeymoon in Paris, using her money. They were back in Dawson in the spring of 1902. Before long he was accused of salting a claim he was trying to sell, skipped out and never returned. He did, for a year or two, maintain an interest in some Klondike mining property and this resulted in lawsuits and counter suits.

Belinda followed Carbonneau to Paris in the fall and returned to Dawson the next year very tight-lipped about where he was and what he was doing. It was pretty much concluded in Dawson that he had blown in all of her money, and one paper asserted that he had even stolen her jewelry and furs. Even worse, she became embroiled in some of the lawsuits brought on by her husband and when a Dawson judge threatened her with contempt of court for failure to appear as a witness, she shook the dust of Dawson from her feet and was seen there no more. She divorced Carbonneau a couple of years later and went on to another career.

About the time Belinda left Dawson for Fairbanks the Stroller moved to Whitehorse and during subsequent years was able to keep cases on Carbonneau's activities only through occasional news stories. They were not edifying. He served a couple of years in a French jail for fraud, briefly kidnapped one of Belinda's sisters, and was an all around international con man and crook. Soon after the start of the World War he showed up in New York with a story about escaping from the Germans, but the story was so wild and improbable that he was locked up in the psychiatric ward at Bellevue Hospital.

How long Carbonneau remained at Bellevue is not known to the Stroller, and in fact the latter lost all track of the "Count" until the other day. He was in his office at the *Douglas Island News* where he now toils and was going through the mail. It included several issues of the *Dawson News* which the Stroller always scans carefully to see whether he has been paid any compliments. As usual, there were none, but his eye was caught by a headline: "Early Klondiker Dies in France — 'Count' Carbonneau Ends Spectacular Career in a Madhouse."

Casting his mind back down the corridors of time to those years when all the Northland was in flower, the Stroller is again aware that there were some weeds among the blossoms but draws comfort from the fact that they eventually withered away.

TWO-STEP
JOHNSON

A Dawson City mining man lay dying on the ice,
He didn't have a woman nurse — he didn't have the price.
But a comrade knelt beside him, his dying eyes to close,
And listened to his final words and watched him while he
froze.

ANY STUDENT OF McGuffey's Reader will recognize the
source of the above parody, but unless the student of
McGuffey's was also a resident of Dawson in the days
when the Northland was in flower he is probably
unacquainted with the author thereof. The author, who
might have been described in his own posey language as
one of the brightest lights of the Klondike nights, was
known to denizens of Dawson dancehalls as Two-Step
Johnson and to the Town Patrol of the Royal Northwest
Mounted Police as a "repeater," the two designations
referring to entirely separate and distinct activities.

Two-Step showered the Dawson newspapers with verse,
nearly all of it parody. He was not a self-starting poet who
could take an idea and work from scratch; almost
invariably he followed a trail blazed by someone else. It
was in the gay hours of the early morning following the
publication of the above lines, and to the accompaniment
of several gallons of champagne, that Two-Step was
dubbed Poet Laureate of Lousetown, the latter being the
common name for the Dawson suburb which preferred to
be known as Klondike City.

If Two-Step had showered the papers with parodies

before that joyous ceremony, he deluged them thereafter. He wrote parodies on everything that could be parodied and a great many that could not, as the results conclusively proved. It was one of the Stroller's chores as assistant editor of one of these papers, to winnow these offerings for the few grains of usable material in each bushel of chaff. But this task was undertaken willingly and performed assiduously, for it was the custom of Two-Step Johnson, whenever any of his lines appeared in print, to call at the newspaper office and invite the entire staff to drop around and have something on him. The Stroller, then as always, put a squirt of lemon in his something. In those lush times Two-Step dined frequently on a bird and a bottle, a combination then retailing in Dawson at between $30 and $50 and indulged in only by those who had made a clean-up at cards or roulette or had struck $7.50 to the pan — and the closest Two-Step ever got to a gold pan was during a lottery one night at the Northern when they drew the numbers out of a pan instead of a hat.

But those halcyon times were but memories when one day last week the Stroller made one of his pilgrimages to the steamship dock, for there is no more reliable institution in the North for renewing old acquaintances and catching up on the news than a southbound steamer in the fall of the year or a northbound steamer in the spring. And it was there at the dock that the Stroller renewed his acquaintance with Two-Step Johnson, although he did not at first recognize the old parodist. When the Stroller first knew him, he was in the bloom and vigor of young manhood, but the bloom had worn off and the vigor had evidently oozed out. Also, his elbows were oozing out through his coat sleeves and when he sat down it was obvious that there was nothing to speak of between him and the furniture. He was, so to speak, but a poor parody of his former lighthearted self. Nevertheless, he expressed pleasure at the meeting and launched at once into the task of bringing the Stroller up to date on his history.

"I'm doing now what I should have done twenty years ago or more, going Outside instead of sticking around Dawson," said Two-Step Johnson. "When you first knew me, I was managing the games at Nigger Jim's and in that capacity I pulled down thirty dollars a day in addition to what I could knock down, which was usually as much as my salary and sometimes more. But it was my custom never to go to bed with a dollar in my pocket, and that has been my custom ever since, although I will admit that in late years it has been harder to come by a dollar to go to bed with, even if I had wanted to.

"It was while I was still at Nigger Jim's and riding the crest that me and Camille got hitched. I guess you remember Camille, the big jane that worked at the Phoenix and owned the Great Dane dog. It was a case of double mistaken identity, you might say. Camille was but recently widowed and it was rumored around that her husband had left her a claim worth at least a hundred thousand. It turned out, of course, that he didn't own the claim in the first place and that it wasn't worth ten cents even if he had owned it, but if Camille knew this she was a whiz at keeping a secret.

"As for me, I was a lovely two-stepper in those days, if I do say so myself, and I was very popular around the dance joints. Also, I was wearing a whopping big flasher of a stick-pin that I had let another gambler have a hundred dollars on — he claimed it was worth a thousand — and that was what took Camille's eye. A jeweler later on complimented me very highly on that pin. Said it was one of the finest hunks of glass he had ever run across and was worth at least four dollars at the top of the market, although the market was off a little just then. I guess you remember the wedding. All the papers gave us a nice write-up and it was a grand affair, even if I did have to stand off the manager of the Regina Cafe for the price of the wedding supper.

"Not long after that, Nigger Jim went to the wall and I took charge of the blackjack game at the Aurora. Things didn't come fast enough to suit me, though, and I marked a few decks of cards. You remember the result — six months at the old Crown Fuel Reduction Works. I can hear that old wood saw yet. And those striped clothes made of bed ticking! How I hated to have any of my friends in the perfesh saunter by when I was wearing those clothes and bucking wood. That was the first time I was ever in jail and they say the first time is always the hardest, but I'm not so sure.

"By the time they turned me loose. Camille had flown the coop. She took off for Nome on the first downriver boat after the break-up with a fellow who had been dealing faro for Sam Bonnifield at the Bank. There wasn't any job open for me, either, and that is when I should have traveled. But anybody could live in those days, as there was still plenty of men coming in from the creeks who were easy to pick. My friends helped out, too; the dancehall frails — Little Eva, the Oregon Mare, Claw Fingers, Step-Ladder Liz, Sneezing Dolly and all the rest — would slip me a five or a ten now and then when I needed it. But things went from bad to worse. Gambling was shut down and the decline of the camp set in.

"Since then I have been in jail sixty-one times, which means I was catched on more than half my tries. And if you haven't been in jail sixty-one times you have no idea how monotonous it gets. Well, it looked like I was just about at the end of my string, right down to the hock, when I got a letter from Camille. Her latest husband had up and died on her and left her with a hot dog stand on the Pacific Highway somewhere south of Olympia. She needs someone to help her run the place and she sent me a ticket to travel on and here I am.

"I don't know whether Camille will consider hitching up with me again or not, and I'm not going to worry about it so long as I can throw in a hot dog when I want to. It's twenty-three years this spring since I saw Camille. My mirror tells me I've changed some in that time, and it's about the only thing in the North that hasn't lied to me. I don't know whether I'll look good to Camille or not. I expect she's changed some, too, and maybe a lot, but she'll look good to me no matter how she's changed, because she's got a hot dog stand and I ain't.

"Well, there's the fifteen-minute whistle and I better get back aboard. Say, though, there's several sporty looking gents on board. I'm going to ask you to potlatch a five-spot, as I think if I have an opener I can start a game of flyloo and make a little clean-up. Thanks! Good-bye."

A BACKWARD
GLANCE OR TWO

THE STROLLER is pleased to note the "Back to the Farm" movement which is now becoming general throughout the length and breadth of the land. Somebody should live on the old farms and the Stroller hopes they will all be occupied soon in order that there may be no place for him in case the "Back to the Farm" germ should bore into his system.

The song of cattle and lowing of birds have been immortalized in verse and song for centuries — by people who reside in cities — but they are not even heard by the sturdy farmer. He is too busy for sentiment.

The Stroller had the fortune to be raised on a farm. He knows the life from Dan even unto Bethsheba. Until he reached man's estate he burned his bed regularly every year the first of April for the reason that it was not needed until the first of the following November. Tall wobbly-legged colts and bleating calves but lately removed from the parent stem are utterly void of attraction for the Stroller. "The smell of new turned loam" may appeal to the poet, but when a fellow is turning it around the edge of an eighty acre field, it is a delusion and a false alarm.

Who cares to listen to the lowing of an old cow that will be docile for a month and then suddenly wake up and kick the strawberry birthmark from just beneath a fellow's vest pocket some morning when he is milking her?

What farm boy cares to hear the bleat of a sheep that kicked one of his jaws off only a month before when it was being shorn? The grunt of a hog has no romance to the farmer whose potato patch has been rooted up from the river until the end of the patch by the grunter. Hogs are romantic only to those who imagine they are born sugar-cured and already supplied with the string for hanging up the hams.

"The aroma of new mown hay" is never raved over by the horny-handed son of toil and sweat who has a pint or so of hay seed inside his gingham shirt and another pint in his hair.

The man is fortunate who is born on a farm but misfortune is his portion if he stays there after cutting his eye teeth.

Anyone desiring the Stroller's share of "the smell of new turned loam" can have it on application.

In his eagerness to get away from the farm, the Stroller took a job teaching school, for a short time, down on the banks of the Suwanee River. The time proved to be even shorter than the Stroller had intended, but although his work may not have been eminently successful, he honestly believes that no tutor ever tuted with a more unselfish purpose or for a smaller salary. But on the whole, teaching might have been a fairly successful career had not the Stroller remarked to one of his largest girl pupils one day that she was old enough and big enough to know something about algebra.

"Sir," she exclaimed in accents calculated to wither, "I am not that kind of a girl."

That night the girl's father and two big brothers called on the Stroller and several acres of the soil of the South were baptized with his bright red blood. The school did not open next morning.

Casting about for something to supply his temporal

wants, including "ham and," the Stroller embarked in the newspaper business and for the next few years he marked his successes by the number of times he was shot at and by the number of hospital cots occupied as a result of his unerring marksmanship.

It is different today. He has been winged only twice in the past twenty years, while the casualties inflicted by him have not averaged more than one a year.

It was in sun-kissed Florida that the Stroller first invested in a Johan Faber No. 2 and started out to lead a benighted people from the sloughs of ignorance and superstition. It was when they refused to lead that the shooting would occur. The Stroller was interested in his work in those days and so anxious was he to make his paper a success that in the event of an issue which did not cause him to be shot at even once, he would go to his room, pull down the blinds and weep over the failure of his well meant efforts. In those days the glory of picking shot out of his legs with the office tweezers was sufficient to offset the physical inconvenience and pain incident thereto. There is one thing the Stroller always admired about those Floridians — when they mean to only pepper a fellow in the legs they never mussed up his shirt front. On the other hand, when they wished to retire a man permanently from business, they never mussed up his legs. They were good marksmen.

If all of the reasons that people give for being in this far Northland were placed end to end, they would stretch the length of the Yukon River and then some. Over the years the Stroller, being of a naturally sympathetic nature, has listened to hundreds of these stories, and many a time he has been asked his own reasons for having deserted the sunny climes of the Everglades for the ice and snow of the North. Until now, he has never revealed that story.

227

The Stroller does not hesitate to confess that a typographical error in a newspaper changed his entire after life and was directly the cause of his coming west and being in line to come on north with the rush of '97 and '98. The printer who was responsible for the error still lives to enjoy the salubrious climate of the country from which the Stroller lost no time in separating himself. It was this way:

Miss Arabelle Bourbon, the only daughter of Colonel Earlscourt Frederick Bourbon, the most deadly duelist of ten Southern States, was married, and, in order that the affair might receive the attention and publicity to which the only daughter of the House of Bourbon was entitled, the Stroller, then the editor of the only daily paper in that county-seat Florida town, was invited to call in person the afternoon preceding the wedding at the Bourbon home to inspect the half-dozen or more triumphs in modistery which were shown by the soon-to-be-bride herself. The visit to the ancestral home was accordingly made and copious notes were taken of the very elegant bridal outfit. As the Stroller was to be one of the groom's supporters during the ceremony, he took time by the forelock, as it were, and wrote a description of the bride's gowns and the many presents she had received before leaving his office to dress for the wedding. In his article he used this expression: "It was the esteemed privilege of the editor to personally inspect the bride's trousseau."

The wedding came off as per schedule and without a hitch, the occasion being the greatest event in the House of Bourbon since the gallant old colonel himself had espoused a lovely daughter of the ante-bellum South many years before. A reporter on the Stroller's paper was present to elaborate the affair, and this was to be followed by the Stroller's personal writeup of the bride's finery. The Stroller did not return to his office after the wedding, the old colonel's special brews and beverages being too seductive to pass up for the prosaic work of proof-reading at three o'clock in the morning.

Between eight and nine o'clock the next morning the Stroller was awakened by an unusual commotion down in the hotel office and in which he recognized the voice of his colored man-of-all-work, Zion. The latter was saying in his deep, basso-profundo, "Ah jes' got ter see 'im as it am a mattah ob life an' death."

Without waiting to enrobe himself, the Stroller went to the head of the stairs and called to Zion to come up and explain himself, which he did, as follows:

"Cuhnul Bubbon am at de offis wid a sawed-off shotgun and he swar he gwine ter kill de hul bunch. He don tuk a shot at me but missed me, being too mad to see."

The Stroller sent Zion back to the hotel office for a copy of the morning paper. One glance at the account of the wedding was sufficient to reveal the cause of the colonel's wrath. The intelligent compositor had made the word written "Trousseau" read "Trousers."

That was more than thirty years ago and the Stroller has not been back to his Florida printing office since. More than that, he does not intend to go until he hears on undisputable authority that Colonel Earlscourt Frederick Bourbon sleeps with his fathers.

The last time the Stroller inquired, the colonel, now past ninety, was still meeting every train that comes in from the North — and still carrying the sawed-off shotgun.

DAYS
OF '98

ON A RECENT evening in Juneau the Stroller attended what was billed as a Days of '98 Celebration, but while he was present in person for this affair, he was mostly absent in mind. The latter was roving back to the real days of '98 and '99 and reviewing life as he found it in Skagway and Dawson and points between during those bright, zestful years when the whole Northland was bursting into bloom. Of course, the Stroller had some harrowing experiences in those same years and many things happened to him that he has striven ever since to forget, but on the whole he is glad that he was a part of them, the bad as well as the good, and the memories of that history-making period are for the most part pleasant ones.

The Stroller remembers two Fourth of July celebrations in Skagway, just twenty-five years apart, and he could not help but reflect that he was there with bells on for both of them, although there were fewer jingles in the bells the last time than the first. In 1898 he was a resident and a participant to the extent that he was a member of the committee in charge of the greased pole exercises, with Soapy Smith as associate counsel. In 1923 he was a visitor and an on-looker, while for a quarter of a century the balmy breezes of summer and the howling winds of winter had alternated with low-whispering requiems and spine-chilling blasts over the grave of Soapy Smith. On the first Fourth of July the Stroller took it straight, except for a squirt of lemon. This last time he took grape juice.

230

As he sauntered along the streets of Skagway during that recent visit, the Stroller was overtaken by a torrent of memories. There was the Pack Train Restaurant with its windows boarded up and a thistle growing through a knothole in the sidewalk and nodding in the wind by the front door, but only a little imagination was needed to picture the tinhorn gamblers, the gilded lilies and all the others who rubbed elbows at its counter while partaking of the tasty victuals prepared by big Louie and served by little Tony. Three doors west of the Pack Train was Guthrie's, where the little ball went round and round and where only the man who kept his money in his pocket didn't have to stand off Tony and Louie for his next meal.

The Skagway city jail now stands on the site of the old Union Church. Six denominations held Sunday services there, one after the other, in Gold Rush days and when a fund was being raised for an organ, Soapy Smith contributed heavily and no questions were asked about the source of his money. But the Stroller was grieved to learn that a padded cell now marks the location of the former pulpit. And on a vacant lot nearby once stood the hall in which the Stroller, his face obscured by a liberal application of burnt cork, once appeared in the benefit show for the wives and orphans of members of Smith's Alaska Guards. He was about to say that this was his only thespian effort in the North, but this would not be correct. The other time was in Dawson when, by popular demand, he impersonated Little Eva in a performance of Uncle Tom's Cabin for the benefit of three grass widows of Swiftwater Bill.

The Stroller could write a mile or more about the chaotic conditions that existed in Skagway in those days and about the multitude of strange and frequently unsavory characters who assembled there. And then he could turn around and parallel it with another mile that

231

would describe the wonderful home life and the stability of the citizens of the town in more recent years. He would relate that the product of four breweries has been supplanted by 5 o'clock tea and tell how bridge has taken the place of faro bank and French Percheron poker. Then he would go on to portray the beautiful home, surrounded by flowers, now occupying the site where howlings from the Nugget Saloon once punctured the atmosphere. The stranger who stops off in Skagway today is not nearly so apt to be "taken" as he would have been in '98, and if he is looking to be "taken" he will not get nearly so good a run for his money as was given the Ninety-eighter. In all the Stroller's early-day experience in Skagway, he never heard a stranger who had been fleeced complain that the job had been bungled. But the town has lost her artists in that line and the man who yearns to be fleeced had better try some other place.

Every visitor to Skagway today should take the trip over the White Pass Railroad both because of its unrivaled scenery and because every foot of its route is marked by history. Just outside the city limits of Skagway is the site of the former town of Liarsville which once consisted of sixty or seventy log cabins occupied by people who required sleep and could not get it in Skagway because of the noise. Mostly the residents had arrived too late in '97 to get over the White Pass that winter and were waiting for spring to arrive, and while they waited they had nothing to do but sit around and "lie" around and that is what they did all winter.

The railroad next passes the spot where White Pass City grew, sinned and died, and four miles beyond that is the Summit, which marks the boundary between Alaska and Canada. The next stop is Log Cabin where the Royal Northwest Mounted Police once had a headquarters and inspection station and where Few Clothes Molly conducted a roadhouse in which "ham and" was the appetizer, the main course and the dessert, three times a day. You could get hot cakes, too, but they always tasted of stove polish. Beyond Log Cabin are Bennett at the south end of Lake Bennett and Carcross at the north end of the same lake, both heavily marked by Gold Rush history, and after that there is a great deal of scenery and climate until the railroad reaches its end at Whitehorse, the head of steamboat navigation on the Yukon River. Neither Texas nor Kentucky has anything on Whitehorse when it comes to plain, old-fashioned hospitality. It was a Kentuckian who said: "We hand visitors a bottle and a glass and tell them to he'p themselves." And the Texan said, "We do that, then step to the window and look out while they are he'pping themselves." But Whitehorse does both, and throws in a big smile.

This stretch of more than a hundred miles from Skagway to Whitehorse and another stretch of more than four hundred miles from Whitehorse down the river to Dawson, while it played an important part in the Gold Rush, was but a curtain-raiser for the main show which took place in the Klondike, where the gold was found. And the bright star of the Klondike stage, as well as the queen city of the entire Yukon, was Dawson, to which the Stroller repaired after he left Skagway and to which his memory often returns when it gets to wandering back through the years. Skagway and Dawson were products of the same Gold Rush, but they were vastly different in character. Skagway was lawless and disorderly and wicked in those early years, and the Stroller remembers it as being very grim as well. The town was full of gold-seekers grimly determined to get to the Klondike, and with a multitude of others who were just as grimly determined to relieve the gold-seekers of a part of their burdens, particularly the cash portions thereof.

Dawson was far — sometimes very far — from being a model for the Young People's Society of Christian Endeavor, but there was a gayety and lightheartedness about its sinning that was absent in Skagway. And while Dawson provided plenty of places and opportunities for the suckers to dispose of their money, the suckers were never steered, dragooned and bootjacked into these places as they had been in Skagway. In Dawson, also, the Royal Northwest Mounted Police maintained a surprising degree of law and order considering the number of people congregated there and the kind of people many of them were.

The Stroller spent five busy and instructive years in Dawson observing the comings, goings and assorted doings of the Sam brothers, Flot and Jet, and all their multitude of kinfolk, including their sisters, female cousins and nieces — at least they said they were sisters, cousins and nieces. The numerous latter contingent arrived with bells on, and sometimes not much else, and they flourished there for a few years and departed. That is, the ones departed who had not landed suckers; those who had, stayed on and many of them eventually became leaders of local society in Dawson or elsewhere in the North.

During his Dawson years the Stroller continued to urge the people to follow his example and put a squirt of lemon in it, with the ultimate result that the Dawson Police Court has all but gone out of business and the police force has been reduced by more than half. The Stroller also points with pride to another accomplishment. When he arrived in Dawson the squaws of the Moosehide tribe invariably wore two piece dresses when they appeared on the streets and there was nearly always five or six inches of bare bronze nature showing where the two pieces did not connect. When the Stroller left Dawson this gap had been narrowed to an average of two inches

234

and even less on days when the mosquitoes were active.

Whitehorse was the Stroller's next stop after Dawson and for a dozen years he conducted a newspaper in that fine community in the southern Yukon and went in and out among its people. And there his efforts along uplift lines, while somewhat slow to start with, were finally crowned with such success that he deemed it his duty to move on to a larger field. He picked Douglas, a thriving town just across the channel from Juneau, but he had hardly established himself there when disaster struck, not only once but twice. The first was the cave-in at the Treadwell mine, which put the mine and much of the town out of business. And the second one nearly put the Stroller out of business, for be it remembered that for lo those many years and from the Everglades of Florida to within the shadow of the Pole he had been spreading the gospel of the squirt of lemon. The good people of Douglas were just beginning to heed this message when along came one Andrew Volstead and left nothing to put the squirt of lemon in. The Stroller has never been the same since and soon afterward he picked up his tent and moved it to Juneau. And it was in Juneau that he took in the Days of '98 Celebration which he previously mentioned and which set him off on this trail of memories.

The Stroller has no objections to these Days of '98 affairs, but what they attempt to do is impossible. While many of us cannot refrain from living over those days in our minds, we might as well attempt to stage the Passion Play on a street corner without a rehearsal or to re-enact the flood of Noah as to reproduce the days of '98 as they were known to Northland residents of that time. Such reproductions serve to entertain the tourists and amuse the cheechakos, but to those who really lived them they are tamer than a soda water cocktail or coasting on a barrel stave.

235

When the Stroller's mind has wandered back to those early years he has often wondered what became of the vast hordes of drifters who came north with the tide and who never mined on any creek, never ran a roadhouse or drove a pack train or performed any honest labor all the time they were in the country. There must have been at least five hundred or them who answered to the name "Kid" and were very irregular in their habits, especially the habit of eating. Hundreds and perhaps thousands had other names, although it is probable that few of them answered to the names to which they were born or baptized. They tarried for a time in the North and then they began to disappear. With the gamblers, the dancehall girls, the bartenders and all the others they have now gone where the woodbine twineth. Of course, some of the former bartenders may have stills concealed in the woodbine, but that is none of the Stroller's business.

Every now and then, of course, one of the early drifters still bobs to the surface, as happened one fine morning a month or so ago when the Stroller met the southbound *Princess Mary* at the dock. This particular bit of flotsam had been known in both Skagway and Dawson as the Wake Up Kid, a name he acquired because he could sleep through almost anything and someone was always yelling "wake up" to him. After a quarter of a century of uselessness in the North he was on his way, at the expense of the territorial government, to Victoria where he could enter a home for old men and continue the same kind of life. On that morning, however, he was sufficiently awake to put up a hard luck story and panhandle the Stroller for a five dollar bill. And the Stroller could not help but wonder, as he trudged back to his office and fingered the few coins remaining in his pocket, how an old reprobate like that kept on living when so many people who pay

236

cash in advance for their newspaper subscriptions die young.

But this is enough memory-gathering for now. One of these days the Stroller will write a book which he will title "Kids I Have Known," to stand as a companion volume to "Bartenders I Have Kissed," which he will also write. In fact, the Stroller intends to set down and put between covers the whole of early-day northern life as he saw it, and he will thereby bring joy to the hearts of those who endorse the utterance of that old bird — was it Job? — who exclaimed, "Oh, that mine adversary would write a book!"